*LEONARD SWIDLER is the editor of
the* Journal of Ecumenical Studies. *Professor of Religion at Temple University, he
has authored and edited many studies in the
ecumenical field. Among the authors included in this work are Robert McAfee
Brown (Presbyterian), George Lindbeck
(Lutheran), Douglas Steere (Quaker),
James White (Methodist), Bernard Cooke
(Catholic), Frank van het Hof (Dutch
Reformed), and many others.*

ECUMENISM
The Spirit and Worship

edited by
Leonard Swidler

DUQUESNE UNIVERSITY PRESS

Editions E. Nauwelaerts, Louvain

1967

OTHER ECUMENICAL WORKS

Leonard J. Swidler, ed., *Scripture and Ecumenism*, 204 pages, $4.95

Elwyn A. Smith, ed., *Church-State Relations in Ecumenical Perspective*, 280 pages, $4.95

Bertrand van Bilsen, *The Changing Church*, 440 pages, $7.95

Leonard J. Swidler, *The Ecumenical Vanguard*, 302 pages, $7.75

Library of Congress Catalog Card Number 67–15784

CONTENTS

ECUMENISM

INTRODUCTION

WHY A COLLECTION of essays entitled "Ecumenism, the Spirit and Worship"? What connection can there be between these three concepts? Ecumenism suggests an outgoing, horizontal movement of Christians trying to reach out to others. But the Spirit, spirituality, seems to indicate an inward, non-transitive movement inspired within the soul, the interior prayer life of individual Christians, by an immanent God. And the third concept, worship, appears to imply an external, vertical movement directed largely by self-contained communal groups of Christians toward a transcendent God. These statements are all true, both of the three words themselves and of the realities toward which they point. However, they do not say all that can be truly said about these words and realities. More can be said about ecumenism, the Spirit and worship, and if a correct perspective is to be attained more *must* be said. But as more is said concerning these at-first-blush disparate realities it will gradually become more apparent how they are intimately interconnected—so much so that to the degree they become isolated from each other, each will become distorted or wither. This, at any rate, is what was learned at Duquesne University between 1963 and 1965.

Since 1961 Duquesne University (Catholic) has annually offered a graduate seminar in ecumenism in conjunction with Pittsburgh Theological Seminary (Presbyterian). The theme for 1963 was ecumenism and liturgy, or worship. The following year it was ecumenism and spirituality, or the interior life of the Spirit. As usual the students were Catholics and Protestants and the guest professors, ten each year, represented a great variety of Church commitments. As the papers were delivered and discussed over the two years the interconnectedness of the three notions came to the fore time and again.

A further dimension was added in the spring of 1965 when the editorial board of the *Journal of Ecumenical Studies* and the Department of Theology, Duquesne University, sponsored a week-long public symposium, "Ecumenism and the Modern World," * which included a number of closed sessions on ecumenism and the Spirit. These papers and discussions reinforced and developed further the already observed interrelationship between ecumenism and man's interior and exterior life, between man's drive for religious unity, his inward life of the Spirit and his communal worship.

Perhaps it would be well to look briefly then at how ecumenism, the Spirit and worship are essentially connected, and what happens, and has happened, to them when they are separated from each other.

Ecumenism, to be sure, refers to that movement toward unity by all those who share the fellowship of Christ, to the reaching out of Christians of one confession toward those of others in an attempt to find a greater oneness in Christ. But it is equally certain that ecumenism does not refer to some mere external *rapprochement*, or even ultimately only to the structures of unity. The sort of unity ecumenism strives for is finally and constantly dependent upon the movements of the Spirit both through the events of the age and within the

* Cf. John Pinnington, "Symposium: Ecumenism and the Modern World," *Journal of Ecumenical Studies* II, 2 (Spring, 1965), pp. 251–264.

souls of each individual. If the spirit of ecumenism does not reach into the interior life, the spirituality, of individual Christians, it will be a dead spirit. The ecumenical movement will be for naught. The letter, or external form, alone kills, but the spirit gives life.

At the same time one cannot be a man and lead only an interior, individualistic life. Man lives with his fellow man in society, in community. If man is to avoid a schizoid perversion of his humanity, he must give expression to his inward life by external means, and at times in an external, communal manner. The promptings of the Spirit likewise follow the track of the divine design of nature, and therefore must also at times issue in outward acts performed in communion with others. One of man's most "natural" outward communal acts is the public worship of God. But if the Christian's interior life of the Spirit must, to be genuine and full, find expression in suitable communal worship, and, if ecumenism must, to be vital and fruitful, penetrate to and become a living part of the Christian's life of the Spirit, of his spirituality, then ecumenism must also find its way into Christian communal worship.

There are many ways ecumenism can affect worship. Christians can learn *about* one another's worship. The abysmal ignorance and fanciful misunderstandings Christians have of one another's beliefs and practices, including of course worship, are startling. Mere reading, discussion and observation will radically change this situation. Beyond this, Christians can learn *from* one another's worship. Not only will each Christian understand and appreciate his own tradition of worship better by studying and observing those of others—this is also eminently true of Christians studying their worship matrix, Jewish worship—he will also begin to perceive the advantages of others and the shortcomings of his own.

Eventually this should help bring about the improvement
—not the homogenization—of each. Finally, of course,
Christians can, and should, worship *with* one another.
There are many levels of such joint worship, ranging
from reciting the Lord's Prayer in common to full intercommunion. The propriety of level will naturally depend
on many circumstances. It should be noted that the Decree on Ecumenism of Vatican II not only urges the
simplest level on all Christians but also recognizes that
the ultimate level is not just a seal of unity attained in
other areas, but likewise at times can be a powerful
means of grace moving Christians toward that unity.

While it is true to say that the genuine inner promptings of the Spirit must find outward expression, the
converse is also valid: external worship must penetrate
and transform man's interior life if it is not to be a sham.
Ecumenism in worship too then must reflect back into
the Christian's inward spiritual life, his internal life of
thought and prayer, his life of the Spirit. The concern
for the separated brethren, the yearning for unity must
become imbedded in every Christian's interior life, and
from there radiate out to his life with his fellow man.

Perhaps the necessary connection between the life of
the Spirit and worship, between man's inward and outward life is clear to many. Perhaps it is also clear to
many that ecumenism must, for its own sake, be vitally
connected to the life of the Spirit and worship. But it
might be suggested that ecumenism is really something
quite new and that Christians have been leading quite
saintly interior and exterior lives for centuries: obviously, ecumenism needs the Spirit and worship to live,
but they do not need ecumenism. Now, it is true that
for centuries the various Christian liturgies have been
the sources of grace for many Christians, and many
Christians have led genuine interior lives of the Spirit

without ecumenism, the fraternal search for Christian unity, having had much of an influence. Conclusion? Therefore, ecumenism is not necessary for a fully effective life of the Spirit and communal worship? Hardly. Our present liturgical reformation has shown us how miserable were our errors in the area of the liturgy and how these errors dreadfully distorted the spiritual lives of many Christians and contributed largely to the divisions in Christianity: one need think only of things like indulgences, a vernacular liturgy and the priesthood of the laity. As to the effectiveness of the interior life of Christians, and the exterior witness to it, one need only look around. Disbelief and scepticism abound and increase. One reason for this is that Christ's prayer at the Last Supper was not heeded: I pray, Father, that they may be one *so that the world may believe.*

The essays in this collection were chosen from the two ecumenical seminars and the symposium to develop various aspects of the three themes, ecumenism, the Spirit/spirituality and worship and illustrate their interconnection; the central thread that runs through all of them is that of ecumenism.

The first group, on ecumenism, includes a description of what ecumenism is and something of its origin and history. One essay probes the outer limits of the ecumenical thrust in terms of partners in the dialogue—the unbelievers. Another pushes out the geographical borders of ecumenism to include the whole world. The final essay of this group illustrates and analyzes the impact of ecumenism on the Church's intellectual encounter with and involvement in the contemporary world.

The group on the Spirit contains four papers on the life of the Spirit, or spirituality, by theologians of greatly varying traditions which have been rich in the interior life. These four traditions include the Roman Catholic, the Quaker, the Lutheran and the Reformed—perhaps ironically, the monastic tradition of spirituality is represented by a Dutch Reformed monk of Taizé. Amidst the variety however two themes predominate: the need for every Christian to make his interior life open to all traditions and also aware of the sin of division; secondly, the necessity of every Christian to make his spirituality one of *engagement,* of profound involvement in the world. The fifth essay of the group deals with one of the most burning problems of the age, interior freedom and external authority, from the approach of the Spirit and authority in the Scriptures.

The final group of essays has three papers on worship. Two papers, one by a Methodist and one by a Presbyterian, deal with motives for worship and with liturgical reforms, undertaken and still needed, in an ecumenical perspective. The final essay presents a world seldom seen by Westerners, the devotional life of the Russian-Orthodox, and it is presented by a scholar who was born and raised in Czarist Russia and has since visited her homeland under the Communists, and who is yet so familiar with the Western mind that she becomes the perfect interpreter.

Leonard Swidler

Lent, 1966

WHAT IS ECUMENISM AND WHY

by Robert McAfee Brown *

LET ME supplement my topic with a phrase unashamedly lifted from Cardinal Heenan, "from diatribe to dialogue." I offer it as a way of underlining the fact that we have come a long way in a short time—all the way from diatribe to dialogue. Just how far and how fast we have come is borne in upon me by the recollection of one of my earliest ecumenical encounters, back long before an endeavor such as this symposium would have been possible. It was indeed, in the Ecumenical Dark Ages—1959, I believe.

The meeting was held at a Jesuit college in Jersey City, and Father Gustave Weigel, a Jesuit, Will Herberg, a Jew, and I, a Presbyterian, were to share the platform. Herberg and I arrived together—I, at least, with more than a little trepidation, since this was my initial venture in the Mysterious Land of the Jesuits and I felt a little bit like Dorothy in the Wizard of Oz, entering the Land of the Munchkins. We walked in the front en-

* Robert McAfee Brown (Presbyterian) is Director of Special Programs in Humanities, Stanford University. He is co-author with Gustave Weigel of *American Dialogue: A Protestant Looks at Catholicism and a Catholic Looks at Protestantism* and was an official observer at Vatican II. He is also an associate editor of the *Journal of Ecumenical Studies.*

trance of an imposing building, and the door was firmly closed behind us, and as we walked down an interminably long and dimly lighted corridor, blacked-robed Jesuits seemed to converge on us, silently, from all directions. Thus heavily, if not indeed oppressively, escorted, we were ushered into the outer office of the Father Rector, where once again the door was closed behind us. We were then taken into the inner office of the Father Rector, and there, another door having been firmly closed, a voice was heard to say to Herberg and myself, "I think we'll just line you up against the wall and shoot you right here."

This voice, I am happy to report, was the voice of a photographer. I only regret that I did not have the presence of mind to ask, "With or without blindfolds?"

Now it is not so long ago that the photographer's *double entendre,* which on this occasion produced two dozen laughing Jesuits, a laughing Jew and a laughing Calvinist (if the latter doesn't seem a contradiction in terms), as well as a red-faced photographer, would not necessarily have served as an ice breaker. And I dare say a Jesuit similarly ensconced in the lair of certain of my Calvinistic forebears might have felt equally apprehensive. We have not subjected one another to the firing squad for quite some time now, but we have not exactly been engaging in love feasts either. For a long time we hated one another. Then we ignored one another. Then we began talking *about* one another. Then we began talking *to* one another. Then we began praying *for* one another. And now we are beginning to pray *with* one another. And when *that* is a fact, no one can safely erect barriers around where the relationship may go from here.

As Karl Barth, the Swiss Reformed theologian wrote to Hans Küng, the Swiss Catholic theologian, about the latter's book on the former: "So then, like Noah I look forth from the window of my ark and salute your book as another clear omen that the flood tide of those days when Catholic and Protestant theologians would talk only against one another polemically, or with one another in a spirit of noncommittal pacifism, but preferably not at all—that flood tide is, if not entirely abated, at least definitely receeding." [1]

So we are in a new situation. How have we gotten to it? Why has it seemed so important to enter into it? Why is the ecumenical era, as William Temple has said, the great new fact of our time?

To reflect upon this question is to traverse ground that is wearyingly familiar to some, but will also be brand new to others. In tracing the route, I have decided that if I am to err, it is better to err on the side of sounding repetitious to the experts than to sound opaque to the novices. Let me therefore follow the advice of the Cambridge don who once said, "When we don't know where we are, it is sometimes a good idea to take a backward look and discover where we once were." He went on to add, "I sometimes have the feeling that in Cambridge we haven't known where we are for the last 200 years." Without passing judgment on his conclusion, I accept his procedure.

First, then, let us look for a moment at this strange word ecumenical. It is, as all are aware, the Theologically Okay Word of our time. Everybody is for it, though not everybody is quite sure what it means. It is simply a transliteration of the Greek word *oikoumene,* from which we get ecumenical, ecumenicity, and that word variously pronounced *e*cumenism and *e*cumenism. (If you want to indicate that you know about that Greek

1. Karl Barth in: Hans Küng, *Justification* (New York: Nelson, 1964), p. xxi.

derivation business, you always put an "o" in front of the Americanized version of the word, so that it begins "Oec." This puts you one up.) The original Greek word was innocent of any theological overtones. It was simply a neutral descriptive word meaning "the inhabited world." After an undistinguished career in classical Greek lexicons it was picked up by the New Testament writers, though used in sparing fashion which is to say that it appears only fifteen times, over half of the uses being emphasized by the author of Luke-Acts. Artemis, for example, is the goddess "whom all Asia and the *oikoumene* worship" (Acts 19:27). In Matthew, the disciples are charged to preach the gospel "throughout the whole *oikoumene* (Matt. 24:24). On a couple of occasions, the term is slightly more restricted, and refers mainly to the Roman world, as when a decree goes out from Caesar Augustus that all the *oikoumene* should be taxed (Luke 2:1).

The word is picked up in the early centuries of the church, particularly to describe something *pertaining to the whole of the church,* the church wherever it is in "the inhabited world." Thus we refer to "the ecumenical councils" as those councils in which the whole church was present—and it is a nice question for later Christian traditions as to which councils fill that descriptive bill. The term also comes to mean that which has universal ecclesiastical validity. The Formula of Concord in the 16th century, for example, refers to the Apostles', Nicene and Athanasian Creeds as "the three catholic and ecumenical creeds," i.e., the creeds accepted by all Christian churches.

But the term slipped into relative oblivion and only within our own day, that is to say within the last half century or so, has it come into popular usage. In 1937 it was used in a statement for the Protestant and Orthodox

Life and Work Conference at Oxford: "[The Churches] are ecumenical insofar as they attempt to realize the *Una Sancta,* the fellowship of Christians who acknowledge one Lord." Since then it has been increasingly used by Protestants to describe a concern among divided Christians for unity; and this is the basic meaning it has likewise come to have in contemporary Roman Catholic usage. In the decree of the Vatican Council *De Oecumenismo,* it is related particularly to movements toward Christian unity: "Everywhere large numbers have felt the impulse of this grace [i.e., a longing for unity] and among our separated brethren also there increases from day to day the movement, fostered by the Holy Spirit for the restoration of unity among all Christians. This movement toward unity is called 'ecumenical.'" [2] Later on in the same document, we read, "The term 'ecumenical movement' indicates the initiatives and activities planned and undertaken, according to the various needs of the church and as opportunities offer, to promote Christian unity." [3]

But the Protestant use of the term has had one further implication. This has to do not only with the unity of the church but with its worldwide *mission.* The church is sent forth, to all the world, to witness to its faith in Jesus Christ as Lord of life. Whatever it does in this part of its life is *also* "ecumenical activity." The so-called missionary movement has thus been a focus of ecumenical concern from the beginning and it is interesting and highly significant that it was actually from the mission field of the late 19th century that concern for unity first began to be focussed. Protestant missionaries realized that it was a scandalous thing for them to export their western divisions into new territories of the world. The Central

2. *De Oecumenismo,* Introduction.
3. *De Oecumenismo,* Ch. I, para. 4.

Committee of the World Council of Churches, meeting in Switzerland in 1951, stated that the word "ecumenical" is equally appropriate for the notion of mission and the notion of unity.

> It is important to insist that this word . . . is properly used to describe everything that relates to *the whole task of the whole church to bring the Gospel to the whole world.* It therefore covers equally the missionary movement and the movement towards unity and must not be used to describe the latter in contradistinction to the former. [Italics added.]

An important symbol of this dual use of "ecumenical" in Protestant contexts is the fact that in 1961, at the New Delhi Conference, the International Missionary Council, organized half a century earlier to give expression to this missionary outreach, and the World Council of Churches, an organ of non-Roman Christendom concerned about the scandal of division, formally merged and became one group, thus sealing the fact that ecumenical activity is to be understood as concerned with both unity and mission, both with the reunion of divided Christendom and the outreach of Christendom beyond its own borders.

So long as that double thrust is clear, we are entitled, within that context, to concentrate our attention on the prong of this double activity concerned specifically with Christian unity. We need only note further, while in the area of definitions, that those with this ecumenical concern are often described as "ecumaniacs," and that an ecumaniac can be defined as a person who loves all branches of Christendom except his own.

Why should Christians of all stripes and descriptions be converging toward one another on the ecumenical front? This must be our next question. Surely the basic answer to that question, one that underlies all other answers and must be accepted as axiomatic, is that all Christians agree that division is wrong—not only is it wrong, it is a scandal and a sin. By no stretch of the imagination can one read the New Testament and find a justification for our present denominations and competing Christian groups. On the contrary, we find such notions as the following: "In Christ there is neither Jew nor Greek, bond nor free, male nor female, for *all are one* in Christ Jesus." Paul tells us that "All you who have been baptized into Christ have put on Christ . . . for *you are all one in Christ Jesus*" (Galations 3:27–28). And—the *locus classicus* in ecumenical discussions—Jesus' high-priestly prayer in the upper room as reported in the Fourth Gospel, "I do not pray for these only, but also for those who are to believe in me through their word, that they may all be one: even as thou, Father, art in me, and I in thee, that they may also be in us, so that the world may believe that thou hast sent me" (John 17:20–21).

To say this is not to attempt to paint an idyllic picture of the New Testament community, as though all were sweetness and light. There was division, dissension, and often sheer chaos, as Paul's various letters to the church at Corinth make absolutely clear. But equally evident is the fact that it is the will of Christ not to divide men but to unite them. And the fact of the matter is that today we are divided rather than united. And that is wrong. The statement of the problem is as simple as that.

This does not mean, I hasten to add, that the cure is unity in terms of some kind of vast monolithic structure in which all difference and differentiation is wiped out. There is a difference between unity and uniformity. No Christian that I know of wants the latter. No Christian has a right to stop short of the former.

This, then, is our present situation. We are divided and we should not be. And today we are at least worried about the anomaly—which, when one recalls the days of diatribe, is even in itself a step forward. For there was a time when we not only were complacent about our divisions but almost gloried in them. At least, we made perfectly plain that the fault lay not in ourselves but in the other. And I think it is well, in this era of burgeoning ecumenical good will, to be reminded of how new that good will is. There was abuse in the past on both sides, of course, but let me draw my examples from some of the things Protestants have said about Catholics. Until 1903, the confession of faith of my own denomination described the bishop of Rome as the anti-Christ. (One only hopes that when the fathers and brethren finally exempted the pope from that description they made the action retroactive.) Here are the adjectives taken *seriatim* from a book published in 1952 by a former editor the *The Christian Century,* describing certain Catholic practices: "odious . . . dangerous . . . distasteful . . . shabby . . . odious and ominous . . . odious and absurd . . . semi-idolatrous . . . objectionable . . . prodigious and preposterous . . ." (I comment only that the repeated references to the olfactory nerves are not in the context of describing the use of incense.) Here is a noted Protestant leader, less than five years ago describing what he thinks is the dominant tendency in the Catholic Church of today.

> So far as can be discovered, "liberal" Catholics exert little if any influence upon the official and binding "line" of the Catholic hierarchy, either in America or at Rome; indeed that "line" appears pointed in a steadily more reactionary rather than liberal direction.[4]

4. See Wayne Cowan, ed., *Facing Protestant-Roman Catholic Tensions* (New York: Association Press, 1960), p. 81.

Here is a Presbyterian writing in 1962:

> In order to see clearly what Roman Catholicism really
> is we must see it as it was during the Middle Ages, or as
> it has continued to be in certain countries such as Spain,
> Portugal, Italy, France, Southern Ireland and Latin
> America . . . [There] we see the true fruits of the
> system in the lives of the people, with all of their
> poverty, ignorance, superstition and low moral stand-
> ards.[5]

And here is a widely-read Protestant journal:

> The Roman Catholic Church, whatever may be its
> other faults, is never lacking in shrewdness or in good
> strategies. . . . The Jesuits have urged the Catholic
> Church in America to label every criticism of the Roman
> Catholic Church as "bigotry." [6]

This is only a mild sampling, and the examples I give
are recent ones. But we know perfectly well, that while
this kind of thing is still around, and will continue, in
some outlying precincts, to remain around, there is another spirit abroad today. The new atmosphere is felt in
many places. Indeed, one can get a significant index of
the new climate even from the political sphere, in the
last half decade. Even now it is difficult to recall how
bitter were the comments in 1960 about a "Catholic in
the White House": no Catholic could be trusted as chief
executive; the pope would appoint all the cabinet members, they would all be Catholics, and probably Irish
Catholics at that; the hot line wouldn't be to Moscow
but to Rome; public schools would die out as all Federal
money went to parochial schools. Why? Because the

5. Loraine Boettner, *Roman Catholicism* (Nutley, N.J.: The
Presbyterian and Reformed Publishing Company, 1962), pp. 3–4.
6. *Christianity Today*, cited in *ibid.*, p. 422.

Catholic Church was engaged in a sinister plot to close down Protestant Churches, and getting Kennedy into the White House was only one part of a skillfully devised plan in which every American bishop was deeply involved. And so on. The hate literature spawned it forth, but a lot of it came from responsible quarters as well, as Mother Patricia Barrett's *Religious Liberty and the American Presidency* (Herder and Herder) so clearly and disturbingly demonstrates.

And it is a measure of how far we have come, that by 1964 the Republican Party felt it a political asset rather than a political liability, to have a Catholic as vice-presidential nominee, while it was felt that the Democrats might have made a grave mistake in not balancing their ticket with a Catholic as number two man. That both the Republican hope and the Democratic fear failed to materialize is an indication, I believe, that we can now safely write off the "Roman-Catholic-menace" theory of domestic politics. There is a change of atmosphere.

What reasons can be assigned for the change of atmosphere? There are, of course, many real reasons, and in the space available we can only point to a few of them. I will arbitrarily single out four that are at least indicative of why it is that we now live in an unprecedented new situation.

1. One of the earliest of these reasons is the coming into being of the *World Council of Churches* in 1948. This in turn was only one culminating point of almost forty years of ecumenical activity on the Protestant front, to which one can assign at least a symbolic beginning in 1910, when many Protestant groups gathered in Edinburgh to discuss the whole problem of missionary witness. By a process too complicated to sketch briefly, various concerns for mission and unity developed out of

the Edinburgh conference, and plans for a World Council of Churches had been completed by 1938. The war intervened, and for ten years the World Council of Churches was, as a famous phrase had it, "in the process of formation." But by 1948, the World Council of Churches was a reality, not a new church, emphatically not a super-church, but at least an organ, a structure, in terms of which most of the Protestants and by now most of the Orthodox, can enter into a new kind of relationship with one another for joint activity, joint discussion, and joint exploration of those things that both unite us and keep us still divided.

The World Council has thus served several ecumenical functions. It has provided a vehicle through which divided Protestants and Orthodox can approach one another; it has provided a means for these groups even now to engage more responsibly in the mission all Christians have to the world; and it has also given a point of focus in terms of which Roman Catholicism can begin to relate to non-Roman Catholicism. Before the formation of the World Council of Churches, it was hard for Roman Catholicism to see where ecumenical activity could begin. There were, as someone said, over 250 different denominations, "sects and insects," buzzing all over the ecumenical scene. But now, thanks to the World Council there is a structure to which Roman Catholicism can relate.

Initially, the Vatican was very cool to this non-Catholic ecumenical concern, and the 1928 encyclical *Mortalium Animos* took a decidedly negative attitude toward what it described as "pan-Protestantism." In 1948, when the World Council was formed, an invitation was sent to the Vatican to allow Catholic observers to attend. The invitation was declined. At the second world conference of the World Council in 1954 at Evanston, a similar invitation was extended. It, too, was declined. Two observers did go to the meetings of the Faith and Order commission of the World Council at Oberlin in 1957, and three more were at the meetings of the central committee in St. Andrews in 1960. And then, at the third world conference in 1961 at New Delhi, five Roman Catholic observers were present at all of the meetings, both observing and, when invited, participating in the discussion, and a new ecumenical milestone had been secured. It is now unthinkable that there would be a major meeting of a major branch of the World Council of Churches without Roman Catholic observers being present. At a recent meeting of the central committee in Nigeria at which Roman Catholic observers were also present, the World Council issued an invitation to the Vatican to set up a joint committee on consultation, comprised of eight members of the World Council staff and six members of the Secretariat for the Promotion of Christian Unity. Cardinal Bea recently accepted this invitation in a speech in Geneva—the first time, incidentally, that so high an official of the Catholic Church had ever visited the World Council headquarters—and the group now holds regular meetings.

So one important reason for the new ecumenical situation is the existence of the World Council of Churches, and the increasingly cordial Roman Catholic response to it.

2. From the Catholic side comes a second reason. This is, of course, the person of "good Pope John." In an entirely unexpected way, this great-hearted man captured not only the imagination, but also the affection of the non-Catholic world. A good many years ago, Karl Barth remarked that one of the main difficulties Protestants found in Roman Catholicism was that they could not hear the voice of the good shepherd from the see of

Peter. Pope John changed all that—which makes it even more significant that Karl Barth, writing after the death of Pope John, commented "What if we [Protestants] should discover that the last are first and the first last, that the voice of the Good Shepherd should find a clearer echo over there than among us?" [7] Pope John's manifest concern for Christian unity, his spontaneous outreaching to the separated brethren, indeed his manifest concern for all men, and his spontaneous outreaching to the entire human family, have created a new situation. There are those who said, when he was elected, that John was simply to be a caretaker pope—to which, now, the only possible response is, "Caretaker pope indeed! He took more care of the church in four years than had been taken care of it in the preceeding four hundred."

We must be fair here. It would not be proper to assert that Pope John initiated Roman Catholic ecumenical concern. It was there, at least in the wings, waiting for a chance to get on stage. But it would be proper to say that he released that ecumenical concern. Before the time of Pope John, there were ecumenical theologians, there were ecumenical intimations being whispered about here and there in the church, but it took a clear sign to enable them to speak openly and freely and without fear, and Pope John provided that sign. One must therefore pay tribute to the ecumenical pioneers—Father Max Metzger, who pioneered the *Una Sancta* meetings in Europe between Catholics and non-Catholics long before the word "dialogue" was on the scene; Abbé Couturier, who really pioneered the creative use of the Christian Unity Octave; Monsignor (now Bishop) Willebrands who was engaged in ecumenical activity in his native Holland long before there was a Secretariat for Christian Unity

7. *Ecumenical Review* (July, 1963), p. 364.

for him to oversee; Father Gustave Weigel, S.J., who was carrying the load almost singlehandedly in this country when it was a quite unpopular and even dangerous occupation, and who in a very real sense deserves to be remembered as a martyr to the ecumenical cause, since he literally worked himself to death; Father George Tavard, A.A., who was writing in this area with incisiveness and courage long before it was popular or even safe to do so; Father Yves Congar, O.P., whose first two books on ecumenism were withdrawn from circulation by the Holy Office, but who has happily lived to see the church catch up to where he was twenty-five years ago; and a host of others. But it was Pope John who indicated to the world at large that the kinds of things these few men in the church were doing in isolation were now the kinds of things that all men in the church should be doing in concert.

3. Coupled with this second factor—the person of Pope John—must go a third factor related to him, namely his decision to call the Second Vatican Council. It is symbolically appropriate that the decision to call a council came to him during a moment of prayer—during the Christian Unity Octave—in January of 1959. Thus, from the very beginning, the Vatican Council and the ecumenical situation have been inseparable. The Council, of course, is an endless topic, and cannot properly be disposed of in half a dozen sentences. It has already been the subject of a hundred books and thousands of articles. But it has reinforced some of the basic dimensions of ecumenicity. It is inextricably wedded, for example, to the notion of reform. If the Roman Catholic Church is to draw nearer to the other churches of Christendom, and have them draw nearer to it, then the church must first of all look to her own reform and renewal. John said this, and the recently promulgated ecumenism decree

repeats it. The first step toward reaching out to others is to set one's own house in order. And that which the Protestant had thought could never really take place in Roman Catholicism, genuine inner criticism and resultant reform, is taking place today. No doubt Pope John had no clear idea of what he was unleashing when he said, "Let us have a Council," nor could he have foreseen the hopes he let loose when he urged that the church open its windows to let in some fresh air. But it is clear that his call to *aggiornamento*—to bringing the church up to date—is one of the most ecumenically important events of the last four centuries.

The ecumenical impact of the Council is incalculable. In one area it is leading to a fresh look by Roman Catholics at the meaning of their church and their faith. In another area, it is dispelling many of the stereotypes Protestants have long had of the Catholic Church, and forcing a fresh look and a fresh reassessment. Many of the diatribes I quoted earlier were distorted caricatures, but behind all of their measured bitterness there was usually some grain of truth. And the Council has rendered most of that sort of criticism invalid because it is now inaccurate, to whatever degree it might once have been at least minimally accurate. (For the benefit of Catholic readers, it should be noted that this is pretty rough on a certain kind of Protestant. Roman Catholicism has always been a very convenient thing to be *against,* and it has always been easier to be against something than for something. But the Council has pulled the rug out from under a considerable part of the traditional Protestant attack. It is not so easy to talk about "one-man-rule" any more after the collegiality vote, and the formation of an episcopal senate. All the old descriptions of the passivity of the laity in worship are challenged by the liturgy constitution. And the religious liberty decree, overwhelmingly adopted at session four, removes many of the most bitter sources of anti-Catholic polemic.)

Another by-product of the Council has been the creation by Pope John of the Secretariat for the Promotion of Christian Unity. Through it, for the first time, the Roman Catholic Church has a structure by means of which it can relate to the rest of Christendom. Individual Catholic ecumenical voices are no longer "individual Catholic ecumenical voices"; they are now part of, and can work through, the Secretariat, where their corporate voices now speak not only for themselves, but for the entire church. The Secretariat has also acted as host, guide, interpreter and shepherd to the Protestant observers at the Council. As one of those on the receiving end of their ministrations during the second and fourth sessions of the Council I must pay tribute to what the Secretariat has meant to those of us who sat day by day in St. Peter's under the statue of St. Longinus, and whose comprehension of the ways of thinking, speaking and acting in the Catholic Church is now immeasureably enhanced because of the courtesy of Cardinal Bea, Bishop Willebrands and their aides.

4. Three things have been cited that have led to the transition from diatribe to dialogue—the development of the World Council of Churches, the impact of Pope John XXIII and the existence of the Second Vatican Council. Many other things could be cited if there were space: the impact of common suffering on European Protestants and Catholics who found themselves sharing prison cells and concentration camps because of their defiance of Hitler in the name of a common Lord they both served, and their consequent recognition that they were too close together in that common witness to permit the divisions of four centuries to keep them forever apart. Or one could mention the fact that both sides have been going

through a period of a renewed appreciation of Scripture, and in this common resource of both our heritages we have found that in coming closer to Scripture we have inevitably come closer to one another, so that Father Jean Daniélou is quite correct in referring to Scripture as the "meeting place of Christians." Or one could refer to the gradual development on the Catholic side of the Christian Unity Octave, and on the Protestant side of the Week of Prayer for Christian Unity, and our growing recognition that those who pray *for* one another must find ways of praying *with* one another. But behind these, and all the other reasons that could be cited is, I think, the recurring realization that penitence and contrition must be our attitude in the face of the way we have despoiled the gifts God gave us.

Every Protestant communion service from which members of other denominations are excluded, every Catholic Mass to which only a portion of the believers in Jesus Christ can be welcomed, remains an open sign both of our strength and of our grievous weakness. For these points, at which we derive our strength and sustenance, are likewise the points which show most clearly the hypocrisy of our claim to be united in Christ. We continue daily to flaunt his prayer "that all may be one." But at least we are now deeply disturbed by that fact, and we realize that the perpetuation of our divisions is a sin against the will of Jesus Christ, whom we commonly acknowledge as our Lord. And when those who call him Lord, cannot truly call one another brothers, something is drastically wrong. We can take a kind of modest satisfaction, perhaps, from the fact that we now are all willing to acknowledge that we bear guilt and responsibility for this fact. We realize that repentance and contrition are the first acts we must make, and that what must first proceed from all of us is a kind of corporate *mea culpa—*

a phrase some older Catholics may still remember from the days of the Latin Mass.

Indeed, the acknowledgement of this fact in an official way from the Catholic side is one of the significant breakthroughs the Council has given us. It was an historic moment when, at the beginning of the second session, Pope Paul turned to the Protestant observers and said, regarding our divisions, "If we are in any way to blame for that separation, we humbly beg God's forgiveness and ask pardon too of our brethren who feel themselves to have been injured by us. For our part, we willingly forgive the injuries which the Catholic Church has suffered, and forget the grief endured during the long series of dissensions and separations." And the Council Fathers themselves were equally forthright, and included in the promulgated decree on ecumenism the statement: "The words of St. John hold good about sins against unity: 'If we say we have not sinned, we make him a liar and the truth is not in us (1 John 1: 10).' So we humbly beg pardon of God and of our separated brethren, just as we forgive them that trespass against us." [8]

When two groups who have quarreled, can face one another on those terms, the terms of mutual confession and mutual forgiveness, then indeed there is a new situation. From this perspective, we could say that the reason we have moved from diatribe to dialogue is because we have moved from contention to contrition. And that is a long way, indeed.

So there is a new situation. We are in process, for the first time in four centuries of confronting one another, and trying not only to speak the truth, but also to speak the truth in love. What can we do with this new situation? That must be our concluding question.

8. *De Oecumenismo,* Ch. 2.

There are many things we can do. In an ecumenical gesture, let this Protestant commentator take the framework of the Council's *On Ecumenism*. It suggests three areas in which practical ecumenism can proceed: common dialogue, common worship, and common action.

1. In the past, all of these aspects of Catholic-Protestant cooperation were looked upon with varying degrees of suspicion, depending to some degree on whether one lived in (to take two cities at random) St. Louis or Los Angeles. But things which formerly were the exception are now to become more and more the norm. Take dialogue. It has been proceeding for some years among theologians on both sides of the divide. But this is now to happen on the local and parish (or as we Protestants like to say "grassroots") level. Provision is made, under the supervision of the local bishop, for Catholic and Protestant lay groups to begin to meet together, not to try to convert one another or to score debaters points against one another, but to come to know one another, to come to understand one another's faith, and to discover how best to communicate one's own faith. As the document puts it, "We must get to know the outlook of our separated brethren. . . . Most valuable for this purpose are meetings of the two sides. . . . From such dialogue will emerge still more clearly what the situation of the Catholic Church really is. In this way, too, we will better understand the outlook of our separated brethren." [9]

2. The second area, common worship, is the most circumscribed but probably the most important: "In certain special circumstances," the Council has ruled, such as in prayer services 'for unity' and during ecumenical gatherings, it is allowable, indeed, desirable, that Catholics should join in prayer with their separated brethren." [10]

9. *De Oecumenismo*, para. 9.
10. *De Oecumenismo*, para. 8.

This permission for a degree of *communicatio in sacris* (common worship) is stated in very guarded terms, but the important thing to note is that doors that have been firmly shut for centuries are opened here for the first time. The advances here will be slow, often frustratingly slow, but if there is one area where it will be impossible to turn back the clock, it is here. Only a deeper sensitivity to the sins of our divisions can come from the beginnings of common prayer. Indeed, more has happened here already than one could have foreseen. In a service at which I participated last year during the Week of Prayer for Christian Unity, a Jesuit choir sang portions of Father Rivers' mass antiphonally to the prayers of intercession, and by about the fourth refrain, the congregation, at least half Protestant, was joining in. And I cannot describe what it did to my tough old ecumenical heart to walk down the aisle during the recessional and see a group of perhaps two dozen nuns joining wholeheartedly in the singing of the closing hymn—which was "A Mighty Fortress is our God." I had hoped to experience that event eschatologically, but I had not really thought it would occur in time.

3. Our common dialogue will continue to expose our differences. Our common worship will continue to underline the fact that even though we sing the same hymn we cannot share the same cup. And so for many the third point of common venturing may be the most hopeful. This is the increased provision for common action. We have many identical civic concerns that we share unambiguously even while still doctrinally far apart. We may disagree about the dogma of the Assumption, but we do not disagree about the dogma that every man is made in God's image and that therefore the color of his skin is an irrelevance when it comes to determining where he has a right to live. We are unequivocally at one on the

race issue, and since this is the point of greatest scandal in our nation today, perhaps it is the place where we must immediately make common cause together. And what we will find as we do so, is that traffic proceeds in both directions down this street. That is to say, as we get to know one another around a mayor's table, we will begin to realize afresh how scandalous it is that we cannot get to know one another around the Lord's Table. And conversely, as we begin to study and pray together, we will find that the content of our study and prayer will thrust us out together into the arena of concern for our fellow men. No matter which end of the street we start exploring, we will, I am sure, be led to the other end before we are through.

So the area of civic concern has more ecumenical overtones than we may have realized. Martin Luther started a revolution in the sixteenth century that drove us apart. Martin Luther King has started a revolution in the twentieth century that can draw us closer together.

All of which sounds quite splendid, exciting, and perhaps a bit euphoric. So let the concluding word be a word not only of hope but of realism. The new ecumenism decree of Vatican II not only talks about the kinds of things I have just mentioned; it also warns against what, in good Council-ese, is described as "false irenicism," i.e., a wrong kind of glossing over of differences, a pretence that really we've just about go this thing licked. Indeed, one of the first results of the new ecumenical atmosphere will be not only that we will overcome some of our misunderstandings of one another, but that when that task is accomplished, we will discover, in even sharper terms, where the real hard core differences are that still divide us. We will find that there are certain things that no amount of good will can overcome. We are not going to resolve the problem of our differences on infallibility, for example, just by being more genial. Nor will we solve them by compromise. There is no such thing as being "a little bit infallible." One of the next results of the ecumenical dialogue may be no more than the realization that at last we are *disagreeing about the right things*. And that in itself is no small gain.

To some, that stage will be cause for discouragement. But I do not think it need be. For in the process, we will have been laying some very important groundwork. We will have been discovering how much we truly do share in common. We will have discovered, beyond ecumenical politeness and small talk, that we truly are *separated brethren*. Brethren, first of all, because we share a common baptism and are thus incorporated into the body of Christ. That we are separated as well, is tragically evident. But it will be the fact of our brotherhood, indelibly real, that will enable us to cope creatively, rather than destructively, with our separation. We will see that there is something fundamentally that unites us to one another that not even our human sin can totally destroy. And we will then be the more impelled to reach out toward one another—not to conquer, not to compromise, not to imperil our own integrity or the integrity of the other, but to reach out in love as far as we can, not really knowing where it will lead. That, indeed, is the risk of all ecumenical encounter, that nobody knows just where it will take us, nobody, that is, save God. And if his plans for us, his children, are slightly different from the blueprints we had drawn for ourselves, then sooner or later we will have to come to terms with that fact and more fully surrender our wills to his.

It sounds like a tall order. There are many times, I must confess, when it sounds to me like an impossible order. But when I am tempted to despair, I project myself back five or ten years and say, "If anyone had *then* predicted what has since come to pass in our relations to one another, he would have been written off as either a fool or a sentimentalist." This has happened so unexpectedly and so far beyond human expectation that we are entitled to believe that the Holy Spirit is in this thing too. So when I look to the future, although what is needed seems, from a human point of view, impossible, I take comfort in the fact that with God all things are possible, and that since the Holy Spirit is indeed at work, we can be confident that he will bring to his own kind of fulfillment even our feeblest hopes and deeds and prayers.

ECUMENISM AND THE UNBELIEVER

by Bernard J. Cooke, S. J.*

ECUMENISM IS generally thought of by people in terms of the relationships between Catholics and Protestants and Orthodox. In recent times there has been a very important extension of this notion to include the Jewish community. It is encouraging to notice that in the program in which we are involved this week we are beginning to take account of what is a very important element, the unbeliever in our midst. Increasingly, I believe that people involved in serious ecumenical endeavor have realized that this is a group of major importance, a group which must enter into our discussion not only because of the vast numbers of individuals who belong to it, but because of the intrinsic importance of the position for any serious ecumenical discussion. Obviously before one goes into this topic an important distinction is in order.

There are two groups of people in the world which is ours who can be classified under the rubric "unbeliever." First of all it is important to remember that many of these

* Bernard J. Cooke (Catholic) is Chairman of the Theology Department of Marquette University which has recently started a Ph.D. program in theology. He is also a former president of the Society of Catholic College Teachers of Sacred Doctrine and the author of *Sacramental Spirituality.* He is also an associate editor of the *Journal of Ecumenical Studies.*

people are believers in their own particular fashion and the attempt to classify them in terms of the fact that they do not belong to any particular formalized religion is not really a valid one. The first group of those who come under this title are those whom sociologists in our day have pointed out for us, sometimes under the term of "the fourth religion." They are those who, whether they belong to a formalized religious grouping or not, really follow their notions of life along a very un-Christian approach to things. They are those who, even though they may call themselves Catholics, Protestants or Jews, even though they may find themselves considered such by their fellows, do not really live in their daily life according to the standards of any particular religious position. For them religion is merely an adjunct to ordinary daily life and their operative value system with regard to man and his destiny is one which functions almost entirely in a non-religious context. On the other hand there are those who with real vision and dedication find themselves forced to deny the validity, the operative existential truth of any of the religious positions with which they are familiar, and do this in full consciousness and human choice, but think of themselves as un-believers. In all justice to the situation, I believe that our discussion must rather basically distinguish these two types of unbelievers and suggest on our part quite a different attitude and approach to these two groups.

For simplicity's sake let us consider the situation here in the United States and treat first the vast mass of human beings who despite overt religious affiliation really are neither Christian nor Jew. These are the people who in a very true sense can be said in their daily lives to be following a fourth religion.

Basically, these individuals are those who are fundamentally uninterested in a faith. The predominance of these people is perhaps not as unique in our time as we suspect. One wonders as he reads history carefully whether or not the vast bulk of human beings have not always tended to fall into this classification. These are the men and women who are essentially tied to temporal pursuits, men and women for whom the important things in life are the satisfaction of their own individual quests, the gaining of as much satisfaction from their own life circumstances as is humanly possible. Quite normally and expectedly many of these do adhere to some religious grouping. These are the people who consider that it is good for a person to have a religion because this gives them a vague safeguard with regard to the future, particularly to the future which lies beyond this present temporal existence.

One of the things that characterizes this group of people, who really deserve to be called unbelievers, is that they assiduously avoid any true involvement in a faith-vision of life. Genuine religious faith, as we know, necessitates an acceptance of a personal God, for a Christian the manifestation in Jesus Christ of the second person of the blessed trinity. Real faith cannot avoid, in the last analysis, a profound personal dedication to Christ, a genuine willingness to become involved with Him as a person. This of course is what our uninterested unbeliever assiduously avoids. For him religion is something to bolster his self-image, something which exists for him. Religion in this situation becomes an almost totally anthropocentric reality and to this extent the very denial of genuine Christianity.

This mass of unbelievers, and at the level of their operative unbelief they are scarcely distinguishable as Catholic, Protestant or Jewish, have little sense of their need for redemption. Immersed in a round of daily activities which are essentially self seeking, they rather naively tend to believe that they are competent to mold their future and the future of their fellow-man. Though historically and sociologically the myth of unlimited human progress has been thoroughly demolished by the events of the twentieth century, these human beings still have an uncritical faith in this Victorian dogma. Without a sense of their inadequacy, without a genuine sense of sinfulness, they are not truly open to the activity of God in their lives. Religion fulfills a certain sense of duty, even seems to give a certain impetus toward good moral behavior, but in the last analysis they do not see themselves as human beings profoundly in need of their redemption which comes from Jesus Christ.

And because they have so little sense of their own inadequacy or their own failure as far as being human beings is concerned, they find it almost impossible to establish any real identification with the poor and the afflicted in this world. For them, sympathy for the poor and the afflicted means a condescending attitude which gives them a certain emotional satisfaction and a rather hypocritical sense of superiority. To them the type of identification which is peculiar to the mystery of Incarnation is almost totally unknown. That they should really feel one in their needs, in their littleness, with those who are more obviously deprived, is something they find entirely foreign to their way of thinking. For them the fact that Christ came to become one of the poor is something that they do not even see in its objective reality.

For all of us who are involved in ecumenical endeavor, this mass of people constitutes a common problem. When dealing with these individuals it is not essentially a question of trying to get them to appreciate the validity and sincerity of other religious positions insofar as they are different from their own. The fundamental common problem we face in their regard is one of leading them to the Gospel. These are people, whether they be Catholic, Protestant or Jew, who are in need of responding to the first evangelization. These are individuals who have never truly been converted to God and who do not have a firm enough possession of any religious position to be in sympathy with a person who holds in depth a religious faith formulated differently from their own.

Yet these are precisely the people who in their uneducated and oftentimes fanatical attachment to what they think is Christianity can be a real block to any genuine ecumenical advance. Beyond the discussions of theological issues on high scholarly levels, even beyond the endeavors of those in positions of high authority to seek some sort of reunion, lies the concrete problem of leading the vast bulk who are church members to a situation of genuine understanding. History proves quite clearly that a grass roots involvement of the mass of adherents to the various Christian confessions will be a necessary thing in achieving any sort of profound and lasting Christian unity. The greatest hindrance in this relatively unbelieving group to any sort of deep ecumenical understanding is a fundamental lack of a truly Christian faith themselves.

So while we must continue the type of discourse which has gathered us together at this symposium, we must also face together the task of asking ourselves how we can achieve a profound cultural acclimatization which will lead these people to Christianity, and then how we can effectively preach to them the Gospel of Christ. Only Christ himself can be the ultimate in a lasting principle of Christian unity, and He can be this only if He is really chosen by those who call themselves Christian. Hence one of the most vital of ecumenical tasks is that each one of us, each community of faith, leads these uncommitted adherents to as genuine and lasting an acceptance of Christianity as is possible.

However, I think the topic we are discussing is really meant to concern itself not as much with the uncommitted believer as with the committed unbeliever. And here I think our perspective and our approach must change rather radically. Here I think we encounter a task which in some respects is much more challenging, much more profound, but at the same time also much more hopeful.

I think the day when the truly convinced and outspoken agnostic was thought of as a completely recalcitrant and insincere person is behind us. One will, of course, find in many situations individuals quite superficial in their education who dismiss religion in a very cynical and uncritical fashion. Such individuals have perhaps read a few things, think that they understand history, and in a pseudo-intellectualism feel it is quite fashionable to be without religion. This is not the sort of person that is of deepest concern or offers the greatest promise. The ones with whom we are most concerned, and there are many, are those who in all sincerity and all intellectual honesty have, to the best of their ability, examined the claims of confessional religion and, at least according to their own lights, found them wanting. This is a group to whom we must, if we are honest, address ourselves, and in so doing I believe that we will discover some of the deepest roots of the very things which concern us in our relationships one to another.

Let me say at this point that simply for reasons of simplification I will prescind from those in this group who are somewhat still allied to their Judaic origins. I do this not because I think that the relationships of Judaism are of little significance to us who are Christians. Actually they are of major importance. Yet the introduction of this element into our discussions adds a dimension which we cannot with justice consider, and so to avoid superficiality it may well be better to prescind from it entirely.

Let us by way of hypothesis make two or three statements about the contemporary unbeliever and utilize them not so much as a basis for adequate explanation, but rather as a stimulus of our own thought in this regard. I believe that one of the things that can be said about the modern non-believer which is of major importance is that historically he has actually developed out of the Christian context. Exactly what unbelief would mean if it had grown out of another situation is difficult to ascertain. We can see a certain amount of it in viewing the problems which have arisen for Islam and for the varied Far Eastern religions as they also have encountered what we might call the problem of modernism. Concretely the unbeliever with whom we are dealing is one whose whole background and development is rooted ultimately in the Europe of the last two thousand years. This is a Europe which, while never fully Christian, has been deeply touched by the world view of Christianity.

To some extent it means that the unbeliever as we know him is specified by the fact that the belief which he refuses to accept is our own Christian belief. I think the very fact that many of these are attracted toward some religions like Buddhism is an indication of the fact that they have felt themselves polarized in a negation precisely by what they believe to be Christianity. Therefore, the rejection element which is involved in their negation of formal religion is a negation of what appeared to them to be the Christian expression of religious belief and practice.

This immediately seems to raise the question of pertinence for those of us who profess the classic Christian faiths. I think we must rather deeply ask ourselves whether the large scale rejection of Christianity by intelligent and sincere men of our day is not a rejection of something which is usually less than Christianity. Must we not ask ourselves whether the men of today who feel that religion is an imposition on a genuine development of the human person, who feel that Christianity is an obstacle to genuine human freedom and development, are not to some extent justified by the fact that the forms of Christianity which they have encountered have been less than adequate in their expression of the Gospel? If the atmosphere of western intellectualism has for a century or so been one largely devoid of any sense of the presence of the divine, is this not perhaps due to the fact that there is a protest of the truly honest mind to the caricature of the divine which is often portrayed by those who claim to be speaking for a God of Christianity? And to this extent is there not perhaps a vein of deep Christianity in the person who is classified as an unbeliever? Would there be the type of rejection of confessional religion that there is in many of these people, if the fundamental intellectual and cultural roots out of which they have emerged was not itself one which had been touched by the deepest strains of the Gospel message of Christ? Has Christianity been rejected because of its Christianity, or because it has proved really to be a very insufficient expression of what the genuine article is meant to be?

To the extent that the position of these men with regard to Christianity is rejection of credulity and superstition it is really a genuine Christian attitude. To the extent that these individuals have by their historical and scientific studies forced us who formally profess Christianity to reassess our positions and purify our statements and practices, they have been part of the providential plan for the internal purification and development of the Christian mystery. And I wonder, to the extent that they really have by their own intellectual honesty contributed to this process, if these individuals do not really deserve to be called Christian? And, if so, do they not form a body of very sincere and good humans with whom we, who more ostensibly profess Christianity, should seek reunion?

To put it even more bluntly, one would ask whether one can exclude from the lives and the witness to truth of these men the action of that Spirit who is the animating principle in the Church which is the body of Christ. Not that one can speak of these men as belonging to the Church. This is the tragedy of the situation. But perhaps in their way they are contributing much more to the true manifestation of the mystery of Christ than very many individuals who with superficiality and complete self confidence are giving a witness to Christianity which is really a caricature of the truth.

A point which I think must be seriously considered by those of us who are involved in ecumenical discussion is whether or not the very problems which have produced the modern agnostic are not exactly the problems which historically have divided us who should form one community of faith. Underneath the multitude of confessional differences, divisions in practices of worship, even cultural alienations which split us off, Catholic from Protestant, Western Christian from Orthodox, there seems to lie one fundamental question: What is Christianity? What precisely is its role in history? How can it make claim as it does to uniqueness among the religious positions of mankind? The answer to this question is without doubt an extremely complex one. And perhaps it is necessary that all the divisions and uncertainties take place, so that out of the dialectic of these oppositions there might come a more integral realization of the true catholicity of the Christian Church. And are not the historical dynamics which have been at work in this process of conflict and opposition the very things which have produced our convinced unbeliever?

History shows that Christianity like every other great world religion has very shortly after its foundation been confronted with the natural tendency to split off the rationalizing of the faith from the concrete cultic expressions of religion. In the West this process becomes more accelerated in the second millenium as one finds the development of theology becoming more and more abstract, more and more divorced from the concrete experience of Scripture and Sacrament, more and more tending toward an autonomous way of thinking religiously, which in the last analysis tends to be more philosophical than true faith. It would seem that it is not an historical accident that out of this over-rationalistic approach there has developed what classically is known as philosophical rationalism, the atmosphere out of which has grown so much of the intellectual world which we think of as unbelieving today. On the other hand, deprived of the intellectual deepening which must keep faith a truly intellectual assent, has there not been the inevitable tendency for the cultic and ethical life of the Christian community to deviate somewhat toward credulity, superstition and legalism? And has not this very deviation tended to confirm the unbeliever in his belief that religion is not something which genuinely contributes to the advancement of a human person?

We know that it is these divisions which have tended to separate us, Catholic from Protestant, West from East. In the anguished striving for some solution to this increasing split between the intellectual and the cultic, we opted for emphasis in different directions, without, at the time of the great schisms, realizing that the questions were deeper than we imagined and the solutions much more complex. Without spending time regretting the history which has been at the root of our present division, should we not now in the fuller light of historical understanding undertake a common task of evaluating this historical process? Should we not study together the ways in which it happened, so that we can heal the breach, not just among ourselves, but between the two great expressions that must somehow be brought together in a viable and living religion; a study which will be an intellectual clarification and a deepening in profound but simple personal commitment. Until we have learned to put together cult and law, life and doctrine, we will not be able to achieve union among ourselves or to give any adequate explanation to the intelligent non-believer, who is thoroughly correct in his assumption that if a religion be true in the fullest sense it must take full account of man in all his human potential.

For all of us, whether we be Catholic, Protestant or Orthodox, a man who is a truly intelligent, well educated and sincere unbeliever is of great value. With an objectivity which in a way is difficult for us to achieve, he can assess religion as we practice it. He can do so according to the principle of the Gospel "by their fruits you shall know them." Not feeling bound in any way to excuse or defend a religious position, he can quite bluntly and frankly place before us the challenge of the rights and the dignity and the freedom of man. Demands laid upon us by the scientific and technological advance of the human race in the past few centuries have thrust toward increased human freedom, both in individual and social expression. The challenge presented by these men is essentially a challenge of the Gospel, if we will read it with complete authenticity.

To some extent I wonder whether the challenge of the

unbeliever could be put so bluntly to us were his own
cultural roots other than in an Occident deeply formed
by the Gospel message. Having in his own way achieved
for his fellow man some of the things which we as
Christians should have done and failed to do, can he not
really validly pose to us the question of the pertinence of
Christian faith in our day? And if we are to authentically
respond to him must we not in our own lives, in our
own faith, probe more deeply into the things which are
really the unique contribution of Christianity? The
contemporary unbeliever is a relentless critic even when
he is not concerned to be such in formal fashion. His
very existence in our midst tells us that something is
inadequate in our present witness, something inadequate
in our Christian living. Perhaps if we are driven down
into the depths of our own faith and life in order to
answer him we will have been driven together to the
very things which will unite us as Christians.

Fundamentally, the challenge raised by the contemporary unbeliever is the classical problem of Christianity
as it confronts the world. Though the precise historical
formations of the problem of faith and reason may have
been inadequate, and perhaps they always will be, this
it seems is the ultimate question which is being posed
for us who claim to be believers. Man is meant to be a
knower, he is meant to exploit the powers of reason and
insight which are given him. Christian faith is meant in
no way to be a negation of this, and the contemporary
educated unbeliever demands of us not just a reconciliation of faith and reason which somehow leaves the
intellectual life of man autonomous and untouched by
religion.

ECUMENISM ON THE WORLD MAP

by Franklin H. Littell *

As THE ecumenical dialogue broadens in appeal and penetrates to the level of local congregations and parishes, there will emerge many experimental patterns and structures of Catholic-Protestant cooperation. Some experiments will fail, and we must be mature enough not to reject the whole commitment to understanding and cooperation on the basis of a single disappointing experience. Out of other experiments which do prove out, passing the twin tests of lively response to the Living Word and responsibility to living heritages, much of the style of life of the Christians of coming generations will be shaped.

Since so much brain power is now going into these new relations, the temptation to reasonable men will certainly be prematurely to give order and definition and terms of reference to the enterprise. But by this striving for clear and fixed guidelines the joyful—and

* Franklin Littell (Methodist) is the President of Iowa Wesleyan College. He is an officer of two German religious movements, the Deutscher Evangelischer Kirchentag and the Europäischer Leiterkreis der Evangelischen Akademien. His book *The Anabaptist View of the Church: An Introduction to Sectarian Protestantism* won the biennial award of the American Society of Church History in 1952. He is also an associate editor of the *Journal of Ecumenical Studies.*

sometimes surprising—work of the Holy Spirit might be cut off in the tender years of the ecumenical movement.

"The Hidden Ecumene" of Our Past

Our gratitude for the openness of countenance and speech of recent years might, for example, lead those of us who are theologians or church historians to conclude that the new day of ecumenical dialogue emerged suddenly at the International Missionary Conference at Edinburgh, 1910 or with the inspired call of Pope John XXIII to the churches at his accession to the primacy. Orderly minds among the Protestants have for long referred to the Edinburgh Conference as the gateway to the age of ecumenics, and equally orderly minds among the Catholics are inclined to see the door to our common future swinging open at Vatican II. And, as a matter of fact, we have every reason to be grateful for these dramatic landmarks in recent church history. To read the writings of a great evangelical Christian like Philip Schaff makes one aware of how he longed for an end to senseless denominational controversy, of how he lived as a scholar and worked as Secretary of the Evangelical Alliance, for example, in anticipation of the age which was opened at Edinburgh in 1910. And many of us at this symposium, remembering the earlier years of hesitant and tentative approaches, thank God daily for the great and good catholic Christian who gave us Vatican II.

Yet, if we look to our history we perceive that doors to understanding and cooperation were quietly being opened before we were conscious of what was happening. There was a Spirit at work preparing us for the dramatic events of our recent years. Missionaries at work on distant fields, opening a people for the first time to the hearing of the Word, have sometimes reported that they were surprised to discover that Christ had been there before them preparing the way. Something very like this is true of our own history, if we read the pages with the eyes of charity and faith.

Consider for a moment the contribution of *Christian missions* in the modern period. While it is true that the great missionary orders of the Catholic Church were already at work at the beginning of the modern period, it was not until the middle of the seventeenth century that Protestantism—with the rise of Pietism and the emergence of the Free Churches—began to show a genuine world-mindedness. The old Christendom, with its territorially defined church structures—both Catholic and Protestant—became strikingly provincial during the first generations of rising nationalism. It was the disastrous encounter with a pre-totalitarian state, during the French Revolution (esp. the "Law of Associations," 1792), which made clear to Catholics the perils of Gallicanism and spiritual particularism. Following that time of struggle, the worldwide perspectives of the Catholic movement were raised higher than for centuries. During the nineteenth century many new missionary orders were founded, and the leadership in Rome watched very carefully lest the Catholic faith become so identified with the culture and special interests of a single nation that its essential universal setting be defaced or denied.

In the same period, William Carey (Baptist) and Samuel F. Mills (Congregationalist) and John Wesley (Methodist founder), building on foundations laid chiefly by Quakers and Moravians, prepared the way for the tremendous expansion of evangelical Christianity in Africa, Asia, and the islands of the sea, during the nineteenth century (the "Great Century of Christian Missions"). During this period of recent history, new congregations were founded among more different tribes and peoples, the Bible and other basic Christian literature were translated into more native languages (approximately one thousand different ones), and Christianity became a more genuinely world faith, than ever before. In a very real sense, in spite of twentieth century setbacks at the hands of Communism, Nazism and Fascism, we live in the times of which the prophets dreamed, when men of every nation and tongue are gathering about the hill of the Lord.

By such means we were led out of the limited perspectives of Lutheran Saxons and Catholic Bavarians and Anglican Englishmen of the old type, to see again the Universal Christ lifted up and drawing all men unto Himself. The powerful work of the Spirit in the mission fields opened doors which we had securely fastened shut in the name of national and Western cultural self-interest. Face to face with Islam, Hinduism, Buddhism, Shinto and a host of animistic cults, and thinking of the cause of Christ on a world map, Catholic and Protestant scholars and churchmen began to discover many mutualities—just as did missionaries on the field in a direct and personal way.

The "hidden Ecumene" of home and foreign missions —or, more properly, of the Church's global mission—is working still in ways that forbid a premature definition of the limits of our hope of union. From Amsterdam (1948) on, the active presence of large numbers of non-European Christians has increasingly shaped the image and the direction of such bodies as the World's Student Christian Federation, the International Missionary Council, the World Council of Churches. Similarly, we were all struck by the presence of high calibre Christian leaders from the new nations at Vatican II, and in the lists of those elevated in recent years to the College of Cardinals.

The representatives of the faith from what we Protestants call "Younger Churches" are obviously impatient with habit patterns and institutional procedures which grew up in our midst during controversies, and perhaps wars of religion, to which they feel no affinity and which they do not intend to repeat. Theirs is another history, in good part, and even our common traditions before the 16th century—of Innocent III and Charlemagne and Constantine—seem more remote to them by far than the congregations to which St. Paul wrote his epistles. They can and should make a much more direct appropriation of the fellowship of the Early Church.

It is worth emphasizing too, as we speak of the hidden and unpredictable developments in the newer fields, that in a number of countries the most vigorous Christian initiative is coming from a section of the Christian movement—sometimes called a "Third Force" or, less generously, the "Spirit-filled sects"—which has a doctrine of the church and an experience of the Holy Spirit strikingly different from those reported in recent generations among the more stable catholic and evangelical communions. The Church of God, the Assemblies of God, the Church of the Nazarene, the Christian and Missionary Alliance, the Plymouth Brethren, and related movements give far more per capita for missions than the larger churches, and they also put proportionately far more personnel into the field. They carry the largest missionary work in countries like Chile, Colombia, the Dominican Republic, Honduras, Panama, Venezuela, and also in Algeria, Angola, Liberia, Mali; they are running second or third in many other fields. Two of the Pentecostal churches have recently joined the World Council of Churches (at New Delhi, 1961). It is clear, in any case, that by the time the full impact of these movements has made itself felt among the older Protestant and Catholic communions, we shall again have from the mission fields a powerful influence modifying our traditional structures and patterns and concepts of the Christian movement.

If encounter with other religions has been one of the major factors across the years to make Christians conscious of their common identity, in the last two generations one of the hidden forces has been the *encounter with totalitarian ideologies and movements.* Not since the rise of Islam a millenium ago has Christendom sustained such heavy losses by external attack and internal subversion as at the hands of Communist and Fascist forces. Like Islam, they are related to Christianity as new revelations claiming to supercede the old body of truth—the best of which they claim to incorporate. The *positives Christentum* of the Nazi creed and the "progressive Christianity" of baptized collaborators with the Communists present theologically the same kind of challenge. So, for that matter, does much which is peddled as "non-sectarian religion" by wellmeaning persons in this country.

Under the new dispensations, a "confessionless Christianity"—without roots and without history—is proposed to replace the outworn structures of organized religion in any of its known forms. As Paul de Lagarde, influential in softening the lines against Nazism, put it: If I am not wrong, then the old patterns of religion are worn out. Only one new form is possible now: to recognize and love god in man." [1]

The only answer to this "religion of man," who became in fact the Aryan "man" of the Myth of the Twentieth Century, was that made by the martyr Paul Schneider of the Confessing Church:

1. Paul de Lagarde, *Deutsche Schriften* (Göttingen: Verlag Dietersche Universitätsbuchhandlung, 1920), p. 82.

I can no longer encourage this Youth Communion Service which has been the custom here for seven years now. This Christmas, I could not hold it in the old way. It was nothing but a disturbance, linked with sport and Hitler service. Worship of God had become a residue, a convenience, denying true service. Now, I have broken the custom. I have called for a Communion Service at which all members will confess their faith, coming to obey the Lord's command and for no other reason.[2]

It would be wrong to attribute the rise of Catholic-Protestant dialogue solely to lessons learned in church struggle and concentration camp. Nevertheless, the blood of martyrs like Dietrich Bonhoeffer and Father Delp, S.J., has in fact fertilized the "dialogue groups"— from the "Paderborn Kreis" to the Notre Dame Colloquium and Pittsburgh Seminar. And it is surely significant that our major concerns in the dialogue are precisely those issues raised by the men most intimately involved in the struggle with the mortal enemies of the Christian movement: lay training, the authority of Scripture, the importance of creeds and confessions and tradition, liturgical integrity, a Christian style of life, etc. The great new factor, working quietly to strengthen the ecumenical spirit and act, is the fact that under pressure the Christians have not retreated into a multiplicity of denominational fortresses but rather pressed forward to learn to live creatively with each other. Along with this, so fundamental to deeper relations between Catholics and Protestants, we may note an increased mutuality of Christians and Jews. The attack of the new political religions, and the appalling crimes of a degenerate Christendom toward the Jews, have

2. E. H. Robertson, *Paul Schneider: The Pastor of Buchenwald* (Chicago: SCM Book Club, 1956), pp. 28-29.

intensified our awareness of history, of an essential quality of true Christianity: its Jewishness.

A third force from our heritage, which has worked in hidden ways to strengthen the Ecumene, which is particularly relevant to the growth of the spirit and act of intercommunion in America, is *Religious Liberty*. In Europe, where the fragments of a post-Christian Christendom still tend to define "church" along geographical lines, inter-church understanding and cooperation tends to take on the color of a problem in international relations. Even there, however, in abandonment of centuries of coercion and violence in matters religious, the most perceptive are beginning to affirm that the highest religious service is a product of voluntary and uncoerced commitment. As Pope John XXIII affirmed the free exercise of religion in "Pacem in Terris," "every human being has the right to honor God according to the dictates of an upright conscience, and therefore the right to worship God privately and publicly."

In America, where the full implications of the Great Bill of Religious Freedom in Virginia and the First Amendment to the Federal Constitution are beginning to be worked out, we have a richer heritage yet. It is religious liberty, the right to discuss religious issues without fear or favor at law, which makes true dialogue possible. There can be no true discussion between two persons, one of whom has the sword of the persecutor in his hand and the other of whom has the noose of the heretic about his neck. Freedom is not, of course, an end in itself: it is a means to Truth. But we are learning that Truth can best make itself known where men may speak, unintimidated and with the open face of truth, in confidence that their natural rights as citizens are in no way affected by their exercise of their spiritual rights as creatures. This is a precious truth, hard-learned across the centuries, of greatest benefit to both church and society.

The "Hidden Christ" in Our Present World

Not only in our recent past but also in hidden ways in the present may the eyes of charity and faith perceive the "hidden Christ" working to bring his brethren together again. We are learning to affirm the lay apostolate in the world, not just the significance of the laity in the church. We are remembering that the Logos is at work not only among those branded with His Name, but also to redeem His whole creation. In the dialogue of the church with the world, there is much to be learned which can strengthen our faith and our unity in Christ.

"*Secularization*" generally carries a pejorative undertone, a note derived from earlier struggles of the churches against hostile powers. Yet "secularization" also refers to the act whereby the world at large takes over and makes its own some property or quality previously restricted to the church. Across the centuries, and certainly among the positive institutions of the open society, many of the works of Christ (*gesta Christi*) have been accomplished in this fashion. Consider such Christian commitments, now generally accepted by our society at large, as these: medical care (hospitals, homes, orphanages), universal education, protection of women and children under law, universal suffrage and equal rights under law, the abolition of slavery, etc. It is true that churchmen have sometimes sought to restrain the outworking of the Gospel. But when they sought to lay hands on Him, He passed from out of their midst. It is precisely the genius of "Mater et Magistra" (May 15, 1961) that Pope John XXIII's first great encyclical declared many of the works of Christ in the world, too often unrecognized as such even by Christians.

Take, for example, the struggle of the Negro minority in our society to achieve the full rights of American citizens guaranteed them by the Constitution and in the laws. There is no more dramatic illustration of the way in which the churches have been brought closer together by a problem on the world map than this. Forty-five years ago a sensitive American Quaker working in India, Samuel E. Stokes, Jr., in a book introduced by the great missionary C. F. Andrews, proclaimed the failure of European civilization as a world culture. In the same period when literate racists like Morgan Grant and Lothrop Stoddard were warning against the rising tide of color, Stokes asserted that "dams against the coloured races, with spillways of course for students, merchants, and travellers, will presently inclose the white man's world." [3] He believed that the basic issue was whether the white man would join the human race, understanding that justice and equity and liberty are indivisible.

In America we are coming to understand that none can be free in our society while another is brutalized and enslaved. A high consequence of this insight was the National Conference on Religion and Race, held in Chicago in January of 1963, which was the first time in human history that Catholics and Jews and Protestants of all varieties officially cooperated in dealing with a major social problem. The follow-up on this conference in regional and local sessions was remarkable. The massed effort of the religious bodies was basic to the enactment of the Civil Rights Law and has been vital in its acceptance by the public. Highly symbolic was the fact that the great demonstration which began as a sym-

3. Stokes, S. E., *The Failure of European Civilisation as a World Culture* (Madras: S. Ganesan Co., 1921), p. 36.

bol of political purpose, the "March on Washington,"
ended as a religious pentecost on a scale unseen in
America for decades. In that high hour, as Dr. Martin
Luther King, Jr. gathered up the spiritual aspirations of
a whole people in the immortal sermon, "I have a
Dream. . . ." Americans were united as seldom before
in their history.

The sceptical might say, not without apparent justification from external signs, that the religionists were
belatedly getting on the bandwagon of public purpose.
To the eyes of faith, however, it is evident that we were
in fact being brought closer together by the mysterious
and often hidden work of Him in Whom "all things were
created, in heaven and on earth, visible and invisible,
whether thrones or dominions or principalities or
authorities."

> All things were created through him and for him. He
> is before all things, and in him all things hold together.
> He is the head of the body, the church; he is the
> beginning, the first-born from the dead, that in every-
> thing he might be preëminent. For in him all the fullness
> of God was pleased to dwell, and through him to
> reconcile to himself all things, whether on earth or in
> heaven, making peace by the blood of his cross.
> And you, who once were estranged and hostile in
> mind, doing evil deeds, he has now reconciled in his
> body of flesh by his death, in order to present you holy
> and blameless and irreproachable before him. . . .
> (Col. 1:16–22)

The passage from Colossians begins with creation and
works back to the church. This has often been the experience of the Christians: that we are brought back to
faith and charity and hope by the suddenly revealed
truth that He is not dependent upon our plans and institutional programs. He does not wait for us, but pre-

cedes us in the reclaiming of the creation to the perfection for which God intended it. The lessons which we learn from a study of the world map of our past or our present are often of this order.

What more, then, needs to be said? Shall we discuss the wasteland of the Inner City, where Catholics and Protestants are learning to work together in imaginative new experiments in the diaconate? Shall we refer to the state university, a needy "mission field" indeed, where inter-religious cooperation and "dialogue on campus" have spread in twenty years from two schools to over one hundred and fifty? Shall we address ourselves to that most difficult of all problems, the jungle of international cooperation and amity, where a clear word such as "Pacem in Terris" has proved capable of gathering men of good will from the most varied corners and responsibilities?

The message is plain: in many ways beyond our present understanding, and in works of mercy and justice and righteousness far beyond our control or definition, the New Creator is redeeming and restoring His creation. While we yet slept, He intervened. Before we ever began to practice dialogue and speak of union, His Spirit was reestablishing our unity in Him. Let us therefore, in all devotion to intellectual integrity and theological precision, look to the time to come in joy and thanksgiving, knowing that He is able to surprise us out of our present theological and institutional limits. For it is by the hidden Spirit of the Universal Christ that we are at last made whole again.

ECUMENISM, COSMIC REDEMPTION AND THE COUNCIL

by George A. Lindbeck *

WE ARE all aware that one of the great interests of contemporary theologians, both Protestant and Catholic, is to translate the Christian message into language and conceptual patterns which are intelligible to modern man. Pope John, you will recall, made this one of the constant concerns, not only of academic theology, but even of the Second Vatican Council, when he said, in his opening address to the first session, that it should seek to express the unchanging substance of the faith in new forms.

Our concern will be with one significant difference between the ways Catholic and Protestant theologians set about doing this. Of course there are many exceptions on both sides, but in general one can say that Catholics show a greater affinity for evolutionary patterns of thought while the present generation of Protestants favor more personalistic and existential ones. Many

* George Lindbeck (Lutheran), Associate Professor of Historical Theology at Yale University, was on leave, 1962–64, to serve as Research Professor for the Commission on Inter-confessional Research of the Lutheran World Federation, and was also an official observer at Vatican II. He is an associate editor of the *Journal of Ecumenical Studies.*

Catholics are sympathetic with efforts to develop a grand vision of the universe and mankind moving ever upwards and onwards to the final culmination in the redemption of the whole cosmos. While some progressive Catholics, not to mention conservatives, are suspicious of these efforts, it seems to me that these suspicions are much deeper and more widespread among Protestants, including the most thoroughly contemporary ones. The Protestant tends to be repelled by an eschatology, that is a doctrine of the last things, of the final goal and meaning of existence, which stresses the horizontal rather than the vertical, which thinks in terms of an objectively future cosmic redemption rather than authenticity in human life and relation to God in the present moment. We see here, I suspect, a reflection of the overwhelming Reformation emphasis on faith in the sense of total trust in the present forgiving love of God in Jesus Christ. Faith has been stressed, and hope has been scarcely mentioned. Catholics, in contrast, have traditionally reserved greater place for the theological virtue of hope, and they have thought of salvation as the ontological transformation through infused grace of individual men. Perhaps this is what makes it easier for them now to think in terms of the ontological transformation of the whole cosmos.

There is, then, a genuine ecumenical problem in this Protestant distrust of the vision of cosmic redemption. But before we deal with that problem, we must say more about this vision and its practical implications. However suspicious Protestants may be of the vision itself, they generally applaud its practical consequences. They like the way it changes the traditional Catholic view of the relation between the church and world. It inculcates a kind of engagement of Christians with the world's problems, with building up the temporal city, for which many Protestants are also seeking. This, I shall try to show, is partially reflected in the Vatican Council's *Constitution on the Church in the Modern World.* Further, these practical consequences of the vision of cosmic redemption open up an extremely hopeful avenue of advance for the ecumenical movement, delivering it from the dead-ends and impasses which otherwise threaten it. It is precisely because of these practical consequences that Protestants, and Catholics also, must take this vision of cosmic redemption seriously, and must ask themselves, as we shall do in the latter part of this paper, whether the usual objections to it really apply.

To start with, I shall not say much about the vision itself. When I mentioned it, some of you probably thought immediately of Teilhard de Chardin, but I do not have him exclusively, or even specifically, in mind. I am rather thinking of a pervasive movement of thought, greatly stimulated by Teilhard, but often highly critical, and sometimes entirely independent, of him.[1] It is a movement which seeks deliverance from the archaic, static, three-storey view of the universe, developed under Greek rather than Biblical auspices, according to which the world beneath is pictured in sharp distinction from a supernatural but created heaven above, and with God at some unlocated point beyond this. According to this older picture, redemption is basically individualistic. It consists of souls, one by one, escaping—or being catapulted—from here below into heaven above. History is relatively unimportant. To be sure, certain historical events, such as the coming of Christ, provide the means for the ascent of the soul from the lower to the upper levels, but most of what happens on earth, whether the

1. E.g., Karl Rahner, "Die Christologie innerhalb einer evolutiven Weltanschauung," *Schriften zur Theologie,* vol. 5, Einsiedeln: Benziger, 1962.

prehistorical evolution of animal species or the material and intellectual progress of humanity, is irrelevant to salvation. In contrast to this, more and more Christian thinkers are trying to conceive the created universe as a single whole, a historical-evolutionary development, culminating in a total transformation when all things are united in Christ and God becomes all in all. In this context, salvation is viewed as the corporate redemption of mankind, indeed of the cosmos, worked out in and through history. Individuals are saved, not atomistically, but through becoming parts of a new and reconciled humanity. Human advancement, even in scientific, technical and artistic domains, not to mention social and moral ones, is not irrelevant to the Christian's hope, but is in some sense a direct preparation for the final culmination, for the ultimate manifestation of the kingdom of God.

This vision supplies the implicit and sometimes the explicit support for the growing engagement of many Catholic circles in promoting what is usually called secular human progress, in building up the earthly city. They believe that the Church, that Christianity, has an essential role to play in mankind's journey towards final fulfillment. It is at least one of God's chosen means for supplying the religious dynamism and the moral orientation necessary for opening up humanity to the coming of the kingdom. The church will do this, not by the dictation and coercive control from above to which it has often been addicted in the past, but by humble and self-effacing service of all worth-while human endeavors even when they do not bear the Christian label. It will do this because it recognizes that God is directing the entire world, the entire evolutionary and historical process, toward the consummation. He is working, not simply through the church, but in many ways outside the church, and so he calls the church to the service, not the domination, of advancing humanity.

Sometimes this attitude takes naively enthusiastic forms. While we should not judge this position on the basis of its extreme representatives, yet it should be noted that the earthly progress of mankind sometimes seems to be considered inseparable from the renewal of the church. It is supposed that if only the churches are reformed along the lines indicated by Pope John, and if only Christians unite, then they will be able to supply the necessary ethical power and guidance which will solve the great problems of war, atomic destruction, poverty, underdeveloped nations and racial injustice. Further, once the Christian family, which constitutes a third of the world's population, begins acting in this fashion, then, so the enthusiasts say, humanity as a whole will recognize that Christianity is indeed divine.

There are many expressions of this outlook, perhaps particularly among laymen. I shall mention simply two books, both of them very exciting reading, by the two most distinguished journalists covering the Council. One, *Church, Council and World,* is by Robert Kaiser of *Time.* The other, *Catholicism, Religion of Tomorrow,* is by Henri Fesquet, correspondent of the most distinguished French newspaper, *Le Monde.*[2]

Theologically trained Roman Catholics, as could be expected, are less prophetic and more pallid, but even among many of them there are reflections of this outlook. Father Houtart, for example, who is the world's leading Catholic organizer of research in the sociology of religion, speaks of the orientation supplied by the Church as making an essential contribution to the

2. Published originally in 1963, Macmillan (New York) and 1962, Grasset (Paris), respectively.

"social evolution of mankind . . . leading to the spiritualization of mankind and to unity with God." [3]

Much more significant, the Second Vatican Council itself reflects the influence of this outlook in a number of its documents, but especially in the *Constitution on the Church in the Modern World*. It affirms that the construction of the earthly city, contributing to human progress in all its aspects, is an essential Christian concern.

> Throughout the course of the centuries, men have labored to better the circumstances of their lives . . . considered in itself this human activity accords with God's will. For man, created to God's image, received a mandate to subject to himself the earth and all it contains, and to govern the world with justice and holiness . . . [Men] can justly consider that by their labor they are unfolding the Creator's work . . . and are contributing by their personal industry to the realization in history of the divine plan . . . Christians are convinced that the triumphs of the human race are a sign of God's grace and the flowering of his own mysterious design (no. 34).
>
> God's Word, through whom all things were made, was himself made flesh and dwelt on the earth of men. Thus he entered the world's history as a perfect man, taking that history up into himself and summarizing it . . . Christ is now at work in the hearts of men through the energy of his Spirit, arousing not only a desire for the age to come, but by that very fact animating, purifying and strengthening those noble longings, too, by which the human family makes its life more human and strives to render the whole earth submissive to this goal (no. 38).
>
> We do not know the time for the consummation of the earth and of humanity, nor do we know how all things

---

3. F. Houtart, *The Challenge to Change*, New York: Sheed & Ward, 1964, p. 67.

will be transformed . . . but we are taught that God is
preparing a new dwelling place and a new earth where
justice will abide. . . . Therefore, while we are warned
that it profits a man nothing if he gain the whole world
and lose himself, the expectation of a new earth must
not weaken but rather stimulate our concern for cul-
tivating this one. For here grows the body of a new
human family, a body which even now is able to give
some kind of foreshadowing of the new age. Hence,
while earthly progress must be carefully distinguished
from the growth of Christ's kingdom . . . [nevertheless]
it is of vital concern to the Kingdom of God. For after
we have obeyed the Lord, and in his Spirit nurtured on
earth the values of human dignity, brotherhood and
freedom, and indeed all the good fruits of our nature and
enterprise, we shall find them again, but freed of stain,
burnished and transfigured, when Christ hands over to
the Father: "a kingdom eternal and universal, a kingdom
of truth and life, of holiness and grace, of justice, love
and peace" (no. 39).

These words are a tremendous advance over the
earlier drafts of this *Constitution*.[4] They express with
extreme vividness the idea that human progress is con-
tributory to God's kingdom. To be sure, they are rather
isolated when considered in the context of this document,
or of the council, as a whole, and yet they must not be
underestimated. Already the new approach which they
reflect, and which was also present in Pope John's
Encyclicals, is having a profound effect on the Roman
Catholic Church. This is perhaps most dramatically evident in Latin America. Already it led to a victory of the
Christian Democrats in Chile in the fall of 1964 which
was unthinkable five years earlier. This victory opens up,
some experts say, an escape from despair, the hope of

4. For comments on the earlier draft, see G. Lindbeck, "Church
and World: Schema 13," *Dialogue on the Way* (ed. G. Lindbeck),
Minneapolis: Augsburg, 1965, esp. pp. 239–243.

a third way of genuinely progressive reform beyond the deadly alternatives in which Latin America is now trapped of sterile reaction or communist revolution. Perhaps the expectations of most non-Catholics and many Catholics, will be confounded. Perhaps the Roman Church of the next generations will not be absorbed in fighting losing rear-guard actions against change, but will be one of the major dynamic positive shapers of the future. Perhaps even in our own country it will be doing more thirty years from now than all Protestant churches together in whatever are then the equivalents of the present wars upon poverty and racial injustice. If so, it will be because of the new attitude of the world's problems which is now beginning to find expression even in conciliar documents. It will also be because of the collective power bestowed on the Roman Church's orienting and serving action by its visible unity.

We come at last to our chief concern. What are the ecumenical implications of this outlook? The first thing to say is that it provides a way of overcoming one of the most serious problems of all Christians in the modern world, whether they are Catholic or Protestant, that of the apparent irrelevance of Christian faith to life in this world. We must later ask ourselves whether this is a feasible way, but at the moment, our concern is with the offered solution. The difficulty is that the activity of the Church no longer makes a visible difference to the world. The Church no longer educates the young, nor cares for the poor and the sick, as it did in the days when all schools, hospitals and works of mercy, not only were, but had to be carried on by the Church, because there was no other agency in society to do these things. The Christian no longer sees in what ways his activity in the Church, his life as a Christian, serves to build up the earthly city. There is an overwhelming need for some way of seeing how the temporal service of humanity can be understood as a direct, and not simply peripheral, concern of Christians. Most Christians, after all, are primarily engaged in this task; they are laymen, living and working in the world. But they have no comprehensive, vivid and persuasive vision of the relation between their mundane, so-called secular activities and their Christian faith, and the results are disastrous. As always happens, where there is no vision, the people perish.

The people perish because their lives are bifurcated into the religious and the secular. The life of society and the progress of mankind are things which Christians participate in, because they must. After all, they are in the world. But they do not see what positive relation this has to what they dimly believe should be their fundamental concern with God's salvation.

It seems to me that one can hear a cry proceeding from the depths of many deeply Christian souls. Do not the scientific and technical progress to which they are contributing, and their struggles for a better cultural and social order have some relation to the salvation of the world? Don't the facts that we now understand the workings of the atom, can send men to the moon, and have a United Nations, however poor it may be, have some place in God's plan for mankind?

If only Christians could believe that they do, then they would engage in the task of building the future, not simply on a sub-Christian level, but as followers of Christ. Then Christian hope would suffuse their worldly ambitions for themselves, their families and their nation and give these Christian humaneness, direction, meaning and force. This is one of the great attractions of a vision of cosmic redemption which sees human progress as in some sense preparing for the coming of the kingdom of God.

Furthermore, this vision, insofar as it becomes pervasive and persuasive, would immensely accelerate the mutual engagement of separated churches. However exciting theological conversations may be, and however necessary the dialogue between Catholics and Protestants which is now beginning, they are likely by themselves quickly to lead to dead ends. Once the interest aroused by doing the unusual has disappeared, dialogue will quickly become a routine activity, largely monopolized by small groups of specialists and only occasionally and half-heartedly engaged in by others. This, it seems, is largely what has happened in the Protestant ecumenical movement, and I suspect that once Catholics have become as familiar to us as Baptists, or Presbyterians, or Anglicans, we shall treat them with equal nonchalance and indifference. The command of unity which Christ gave to his disciples can so easily be sidetracked. After all, we are also obligated to be faithful to the truth as we see it, and consequently the predominantly theological road to unity will reach an impasse once we have clarified what seemed to us our irreducible differences.

However, as the Second Vatican Council's decree on ecumenicism and as the World Council statements repeatedly have said, theology is not the only road to union. Cooperation between the churches on the practical level is also important. However, the difficulty is that the church is not particularly interested in the great problems of mankind. The problems of underdeveloped nations or of the fight against racial injustice, for example, have a rather low priority on the agenda of ecclesiastical institutions. In part, this is the result of sinful human inertia, but in part also, it results from the three-storey picture of the universe with which the churches and their members still operate. According to this, the Church's job is to preach a salvation which is radically discontinuous with earthly progress. To be sure, insofar as men are saved by the grace of God, they will act with faith and love, with Christian motivations in the world. However, this is a kind of by-product. Further, the Church's chief concern with the social order is that it provide appropriate conditions for the free preaching of the Gospel and for the nurture of Christian souls. Justice and love are clearly important from this point of view, but the Church sets no great store by human progress as this is normally understood by normal men. It is not concerned with technical and scientific advances, with artistic achievements or with the social and political unification of humanity. Now if this attitude were reversed, if the churches really came to believe that it was their Christian duty to engage in the construction of a better world, the world of higher intellectual and material, social and cultural accomplishments, because in this way the kingdom of God was being prepared for, then we could expect their activities in these domains greatly to increase. Further, the importance of united action would become evident. In our society, with its pluralistic features, it is only through united action that the churches can exercise any real effect upon public life. It is only thus that they can contribute effectively to the struggles against racial injustice and poverty, and for international peace and a richer educational and cultural life. If the churches believe that this kind of activity is really important, then they will come to find ways of doing it, and these ways must be ecumenical. It is through this kind of cooperation in the public domain that the churches will be brought into real interaction with each other, that they will be forced seriously to consider their theological differences, that they will be forced to take seriously the problems of their visible disunity. Unless the churches begin acting together in such a way that their visible disunity becomes a serious practical disadvantage, they will not be driven to seek every possible way of uniting under God.

However, it is time now to return to the very real difficulties involved in this vision of cosmic redemption and its practical consequences. Perhaps the best way of getting into the problem is to say that the developments which I have tried to sketch sound suspiciously, to most Protestants, like the social gospel which was so influential in American Protestantism for several decades around the turn of the century and whose after-effects are still with us. By and large, the social gospelers were modern men interested in adapting faith to the contemporary modes of thought. They shared the evolutionary optimism of the late nineteenth century. They thought that mankind through scientific and social advances was moving ever upwards and onwards to higher and higher levels of perfection. Christianity was making an essential moral contribution to this development. As mankind progressed, Christianity would be universally accepted and the kingdom of God would be ushered in. This would happen sooner rather than later. "The world can be won for Christ in this generation" was the slogan of the missionary student volunteer movement a mere fifty years ago. As we know, this mood of confident optimism was utterly shattered by two world wars, the great depression, the abysmal bestiality of Nazism and the ruthless utopianism of communism, as well as by American atomic bombings. These have served to remind us that man is capable of just as great, and perhaps greater, wickedness in our modern world than in past generations. Protestant theologians have had their fingers painfully burned within living memory, and they are inclined to look with deepest suspicion on anything which resembles the illusory optimism of the social gospel.

Now it must be admitted that a good many of the objections against the social gospel apply also to some versions of cosmic redemption, perhaps particularly to Teilhard's, as well as to some of the practical attitudes which these have inspired. This is evident, I hope, from the description that I have already given. However, what I shall try to do is to show that, for at least many of these defects, there is no necessity in the cosmic vision itself. It may and is being developed in such ways that it escapes the usual accusations. We cannot go into this in detail. I shall simply list some of these accusations, and then make some remarks on how they can be avoided.

An evolutionary vision of cosmic redemption is accused of being derived from science rather than revelation; secondly, of underestimating man's sinfulness and of trusting in natural process of evolution and human effort rather than God; thirdly, of forgetting that according to the biblical picture the struggle with evil will continue and even intensify until the end of time; fourthly, of ignoring that there is a radical discontinuity between all earthly, human history, and eschatological fulfillment. All of these objections are valid against the early, nineteenth century forms of Christian evolutionary thinking. Do they also apply to the contemporary variety?

The fundamental difference between these present and past forms of theology is, of course, that the first affirms an infinitely transcendent fulfillment of the entire universe, while the social gospel, in contrast, thought in terms of a rather prosaic, inner-worldly kingdom of God, a social order of justice, love and prosperity which, in some respects, had remarkable similarities to the bourgeois society of a past century.

Going into more detail, we might first point out that the vision of cosmic redemption does not need to rest upon the shifting sands of changing scientific theories. It can be firmly grounded in the Bible, especially, perhaps Ephesians and Colossians. In the second place, it is clear that the biblical authors regard the new heaven and the new earth for which they hope as much more integrally related to the present heaven and earth than has been recognized during the past centuries of Christian history which have been influenced by the Greek three-storey view of the world. The new heaven and the new earth are, in the biblical view, the restoration, elevation and transformation of the reality which we experience. This is affirmed, for instance, by the doctrine of the resurrection of the body, which emphasizes that it is physical existence and this physical cosmos which will be glorified. In the third place, it can be argued that the interpretation of this biblical vision in terms of a modern evolutionary world picture is not only possible for Christians, but is commanded, for instance, by St. Paul's injunction to bring all thoughts into captivity to Christ. Biological evolution and human progress of a certain kind are facts which most contemporary Christians fully accept, and so they are obligated to try to discern what place these presumed facts have in God's creative purpose and providential guidance of His world. Fourthly, because it is this world as a whole which God will transform, one must say that all the positive aspects of God's progressively unfolding creation including, so to speak, the physical, cultural and intellectual values, not simply the narrowly moral or religious ones, will enter into the eschatological kingdom. In contributing, therefore, to human progress men are God's instruments in supplying, one might say, material for the eschaton.

So far we have not answered what for many people is the fundamental objection, that the apocalyptic visions of the Bible suggest, not that the world is getting progressively better and better, but rather that the conflict between good and evil will constantly intensify until it culminates in a final cataclysm. However, there is no contradiction between this apocalyptic vision and recognizing the importance of progress in preparing the way for God's redemption of the world. Every human advance increases the possibilities of evil as well as good. The corruption of the best is the worst. Communist ruthlessness is the by-product of a largely Hebrew-Christian vision of the good society, of an attempt to bring heaven to earth; Nazi barbarism was worse than any of the barbarisms of the past; the most ghastly of all weapons is the result of the most splendid achievements of science. However, we must always remember that as the possibilities of evil increase, so also do the possibilities for good. And that, in the cosmic vision of redemption, is precisely why God creatively wills human progress. Through the possibilities of ever greater good which it provides, he is creating the conditions for the coming of his Kingdom.

Perhaps it is helpful here to think in terms of an analogy between the preparation of Israel and the world for the first coming of Christ two thousand years ago in Palestine and the preparation now taking place for the Second Coming of Christ. The New Testament is quite clear that the earlier period is to be viewed as preparation for the Messiah. From the modern perspective this would mean that the billions of years of physical and biological evolution and thousands of years of Israelite history created the social and religious preconditions. The early church added to this that the history of other races, Greek philosophy and Roman peace, also belonged to the *praeparatio Evangelica*. Until all this physical, intellectual and political, as well as religious, progress had been made, the world was not ready for Christ. He came in the fullness of time and as the fulfillment of all times. Yet he also came discontinuously, from above, as an eruption of the kingdom of God into history, not as an ordinary emergent novelty.

It can be argued that an analagous pattern applies to our interim period. Exploration of the atom, the sending of men to the moon, the ever-increasing physical and cultural unification of mankind are perhaps in a somewhat similar fashion creating the conditions for the final manifestation of the kingdom of God. The world is not getting better in any unambiguous way. And yet perhaps even our ambiguous so-called secular achievements are being used by God to prepare the way for the consummation, just as he used the Greeks and the political accomplishments of the Romans to prepare for the coming of the kingdom in the person of Jesus. Perhaps he is also using often equally ambiguous religious developments, such as the ecumenical movement, just as he used and is using his covenant people, the Jews. We, of course, cannot discern exactly how human and religious developments contribute to God's plan any more than could the people of Israel before Christ, but perhaps it is proper for Christians to believe that in hoping and working for such progress they are hoping and working for the establishment of God's preconditions for the fulfillment, the consummation, of all things.

I have cast these suggestions in a hypothetical mood because I am not absolutely sure that they answer all our problems. I am particularly troubled by the possibility that this kind of futuristic, realistic, evolutionary eschatology may, for some people, be simply a modernized version of ancient Chiliasm or more recent Millenialist sectarianism. There is danger that this concentration on the temporal future will distract attention from the one thing necessary. The one thing necessary, of course, is our present relation to God. What does the glorious future of the cosmos or even its present preparation profit a man if he lose his own soul? In other words, to use the phraseology of modern existentialism, this talk of the future eschaton may well prove to be a way of escaping from the eschatological present, from the problem of authentic existence here and now. I am enough of a Lutheran to believe that the greatest thing in heaven and earth is the forgiveness of sins, and cannot help but read with dismay the offhand remarks, even of Catholic theologians with whom I am in great sympathy, to the effect that salvation is not simply a matter of the forgiveness of sins but rather of the divinization of man. Karl Rahner, for example, has said this,[5] and in his case I am sure that what is involved is not so much a fundamental disagreement but rather what, from my point of view, is an extraordinarily limited use of the phrase "forgiveness of sins." The forgiveness of sins, after all, is the breaking down of the middle wall of partition between man and God, it is the reconciliation of humanity to God, it is their unification in personal love and communion. Surely, this is the essence of what is meant by divinization, and this, to be sure, is something with which Karl Rahner agrees.

Nevertheless, Protestants need to take seriously the question of whether the forgiveness of sins does not also have its cosmic dimensions. Do not faith and love also involve a realistic hope in an objectively real fulfillment? Does not often authenticity in the present require hope for even the mundane future? How can men fail to be

5. *Nature and Grace,* London: Sneed & Ward, 1963, p. 24.

alienated from their work unless they believe in its ultimate significance? And how can the Christian fail to be alienated from his participation in the temporal and material progress of mankind unless he is convinced that in some fashion here also, and not simply in his interpersonal relations, he is working for something which contributes to the eternal kingdom?

There are many problems which we have left untouched. We have not spoken of the relation of the Church's central activities of worship, of preaching the gospel, and of celebrating the sacraments to its engagement in temporal activities. We have not dealt with the dangers of the obsession with the worldly power which inevitably increases when the Church visibly unites and increases the effectiveness of its collective social and cultural action. We have not spoken of how these dangers can be countered by the Church patterning its action on the humble service of the one whom it calls Master. These matters will have to be left for other occasions. We have wished to raise only one question. Does not the grand vision of God working out the salvation of his universe through all the processes of history and of nature provide precisely the framework within which the Church can see that its task is the humble and united service of the world even in its temporal and so-called secular progress? In so far as it really sees this, it will thereby testify not only by word and worship, but by all its being in action, to the Christ who emptied himself, who took upon himself the form of the servant, and thereby is both the beginning and the end of history.

THE SPIRIT

THE HEART OF ECUMENISM

by William McNamara, O.C.D.*

THE HOPE of ecumenism is that we will be compelled by the Spirit Who animates the Church to witness to the Truth: "So that," in the words of Christ, "they may be one just as We are: I in union with them and You with Me." But grace perfects nature. This means that wherever God finds a good, decent human nature in rapport with himself, He sanctifies it. Only a good, decent human nature perfected by grace will ever be compelled by the Spirit Who animates the Church to witness to the Truth.

Therefore, the heart of ecumenism is the effort of the Churches to humanize their members: the essential and consuming mission of Christianity is to do what Christ came to do: "I come that you may have life and have it more abundantly." And so, like Christ, Christianity must get involved not with religion but with man and man's world. This is true also of non-Christian religions. Their purpose is to ready man for the gift of God: the fulness of life. It is when we—as religious leaders—

* William McNamara, O.C.D. (Roman Catholic), founder and director of the Spiritual Life Institute of America at Sedona, Arizona (whose board is comprised of Catholics, Protestants and Jews), is the author of *The Art of Being Human* and the founder and editor of the theological quarterly *Spiritual Life*.

move out and away from this creative center of religion, the heart of ecumenism, that we become divisive and fragmented.

My contention is this: if we would all concentrate on becoming human, which is the surest and deepest and most unifying common denominator we have, the possibilities of unity would be heightened immeasurably. Our lives today have become godless to the point of almost complete vacuity. The great task in the education of present and future generations is to restore man to a state of fitness for God. The Church's mission in the world today is a desperate one of helping to create conditions in which man can return to himself, recover something of his lost humanity, as a necessary preparation for his ultimate return to God. But as he now is, alienated, void, internally dead, modern man has in effect no capacity for God.

Are we meeting the needs of man by our competitive and parochial endeavors, our baroque glamorizing of the mysteries of faith, our dramatic banalities, the false glitter of our new apologetic techniques? Instead of facing together the big issues of the world, and coming to terms with stark reality, the separated Churches—my own included—concern themselves with the hunger of "pious souls" for their own satisfaction. Instead of the difficult, exploratory and diagnostic work of seeking modern man in his spiritual wilderness with all its baffling problems—an involvement that would surely tend to unite us—our Churches, especially our Church leaders, i.e., bishops, are exhausted by parochial trivia and stultified by conventional, routine piety.

Man has gradually become inhuman and yet we are preoccupied with relatively insignificant details of ritual, organization, ecclesiastical bureauracy, the brick and mortar race, and the niceties of law. We who teach religion and preach the truths of faith to an unbelieving world are often more concerned with proving ourselves right than with really discovering and satisfying the spiritual hunger of those to whom we speak. We are too ready to assume that we know, better than the unbeliever, what ails him. We take it for granted that the only answer he needs is contained in formulas so familiar to us that we utter them without thinking. And, if we fail to reach him thus, it is *his* perversion!

We do this sort of thing among ourselves, too. Controversial theology can be distracting. By controversial theology I mean discussions on those doctrines which divided Christianity at the time of the Reformation. Theological discussions should revolve around the question that is of primary importance to all believing Christians today, namely, how modern man can live and present authentic Christianity to the non-Christians in their own country so that it does not appear to them as a spiritual and ceremonial museum piece. This is the urgent task of all confessions. Common effort on this problem will contribute more to Christian unity than a concentration on the old questions of controversial theology.

Man must be educated to resume his proper status of manhood and religion must be taught intensively by truly religious teachers. The profession has fallen into disrepute because of our superficial, fragmented, and desperate efforts. What is needed is not Catholic, Protestant, Jewish, or Buddhistic good will and piety but truly whole men—holy men—ready to cooperate, pooling their resources, marshaling their forces in an all-out effort for the betterment of mankind and human order. For this purpose, it seems to me, we need a worldly-grounded theology fixed on two focal points: man and God. I will refer to these two points as theological humanism and theological mysticism, respectively.

Theological Humanism

Christian humanism is that doctrine which urges man to find in the integral acceptance of Christianity the highest accomplishment of his humanity. It is interesting to note that, when God decided to unite Himself hypostatically with one of His creatures, He bypassed the hierarchy of archangels and angels, that world of pure spirits, and entered into the darkness of the universe, into the darkness of a woman's womb and became flesh of her flesh, and bone of her bone so that the Church could put those remarkable words of Scripture into the mouth of our Lady: "I am black but beautiful"; I am black because I am made out of the materiality of the earth and I am beautiful precisely because I am black, for, if I did not have a material body, I could never become the Mother of God.

That was the first singular instance of Christian humanism in the world. God affirming once and for all the inherent goodness of the universe, of the world, of nature, of humanity, of the flesh. And in the life of our Lady there was never any negating of her human fulness, no thwarting of her initiative, no dwarfing of her personality; but a gradual gracious, charming integration of her whole human being.

Christian humanism is a philosophy of life—a philosophy that answers the everlasting question: What is the purpose of human life? It is a common question; so common it is barely noticed, hardly ever answered; almost never faced squarely and seriously. The fact is that most people have the wrong idea of the purpose of life. Ask ten men this basic question and nine of them will say:

"The purpose of life is to save my soul." And they will back it up with dozens of catechisms. But it is wrong. I do not say it is heretical. It is certainly not, strictly speaking, a theological error. It has, in fact, some good but very limited, partial theological sense. However, it is the psychological ramifications of such an answer in the actual life of a real human being that are distressing.

Imagine what would happen, for instance, if you really believed that the first and foremost purpose of life was to save your own soul, and you set out seriously to do it. All your thoughts, desires, and actions, even your service to your neighbor, even your lovemaking, would be, primarily, for your own sake. See what is happening? You are becoming an egoistic horror; and in the name of religion. You are losing your capacity to judge things objectively, to respond to value other than your own, to act selflessly, to love. You come to the aid of your hungry, needy neighbor not because he is good, a living witness of Christ, an image of God; but rather for what you get out of this service, namely, merit, growth in grace, assurance of your own salvation.

There are many pious people who stifle their love and spoil their lives by an inordinate desire to save their own souls. You must save your soul. This is vastly important; "What doth it profit a man to gain the whole world if he loses his own soul!" But the point is: you save your soul best, without any unwholesome, un-Christian psychological effects, by setting out, first of all, to fulfill the purpose of life.

What is this purpose, then, if not the salvation of one's soul? The Word of God cannot be improved. If you read the Gospel, you will notice that whenever our Lord speaks of the purpose of life it is never in terms of "getting" anything: moral improvement, perfection, or salvation. It is always in the terms of "giving"—GIVING HONOR

AND GLORY TO GOD. That is the purpose of life. The by-product of zest and zeal for God's glory is perfection, holiness, and, certainly, salvation. That is what our Lord meant when He said that we must seek first His kingdom, and everything else would unfold inevitably, graciously. And when He said that we must lose our lives in order to save them, He was talking about the same thing.

In other words, we must be so concerned about God and His kingdom, His glory, His will, that we come very close to forgetting about ourselves. We must be so taken up with our Father's business, that we would never think of setting up a pokey little business of our own. And so our petty little problems get swallowed up in the unrelenting, consuming pursuit of God's honor and glory. Giving honor and glory to God is the purpose of all life—vegetable and animal as well as human. Trees give glory to God by being good, decent trees. Dogs give glory to God by being as doggy as possible. Humans give glory to God by being human—by being as human as possible.

On that day that we become as perfectly human as we can in this world, then we shall be saints—live saints, not dead saints; human saints, not odd, sour-faced, or inhuman saints. If, here and now, we are not saints, it is only because we are not human enough. I think the best definition of a saint is: a whole man—holy. That is why it is true to say that if a man does not become a saint he is a failure.

Now, what is it that distinguishes us from every other animal in the world and really makes us human? It is the spiritual powers of knowing and loving. When these powers are fully exercised and satisfied, then we are completely humanized. But God is the only object that can fully exercise and satisfy the human capacity for knowledge and love. Therefore, it is loving knowledge of God and His creation that makes a saint; not flight from the world, multiplication of devotions, or even moral rectitude.

The sanctifying process is a humanizing process. It is the progressive enlightenment of the mind and enlargement of the heart. It is to know God so well that you fall in love with Him—and once you know Him you have to love him: He is so infinitely lovable—and it is this positive, outgoing, unselfish love that drives you to avoid evil and practice virtue, and do penance. But above all, it makes you human—kind, joyous, enthusiastic, adventurous, uproariously happy, relentlessly apostolic.

Look at us, with our refined, precise program of spirituality and our scientific studies of religion, our accumulated experience of centuries, our advanced education, our psychological discoveries; all this plus spiritual books, retreats, meditations, and liturgical exercises—and still, with all this machinery at our disposal and plentiful evidence of good will, we do not find many really great, convincing Christians among us. Not many saints. Why not? I venture to say it is due, principally, to one simple cause: we are afraid to live fully. We are not human enough. No, right from the outset, from an utterly false notion of piety, we dare not let ourselves become human beings. A human being is made, not born.

When we become perfectly human, we are saints. But we do not become perfectly human by our own power alone. Christ came to divinize us, make us like God, enrich us with divine life, life that would never diminish or grow dull with age or boredom. The Church, the contemporary Christ, has the same purpose; so has grace, the gift of divine life, supervitality. It is a mistake to think the only purpose of grace is to help us keep the commandments, to make us better, improved men, with nicer manners. To think this way is to miss the whole point of what our Lord means by being reborn, of all that St. Paul has to say about "newness of life," being "alive to God," and "all aglow with the Spirit." The purpose of grace is to make us richly, exuberantly alive.

We must not forget that grace needs a deep, reliable, healthy, natural ground if it is to take root and bear fruitfully, that otherwise the supernatural remains in the air, is unnatural, a phantom without strength or life-blood.

And so there has to be a basic hunger and thirst, a spontaneous zest for life. Have you ever noticed whom it is our Lord takes special pains to commend? The pagan centurion, the woman of the streets. Who is the only man in the world to whom God ever promised heaven? A thief. And the heroes of His favorite parables are the prodigal son and the good Samaritan. It is the Scribes and Pharisees, with their strict but heartless fidelity to the Law, whom He denounces. He calls them "whited sepulchres." Exactly: they were closed and opposed to lighthearted joy and mirth, to love, freedom, and good fellowship that ought to (indeed, must!) characterize the children of God.

In this context Bernanos' question makes impressive good sense: "Won't damnation be the tardy discovery, the discovery much too late, after death, of a soul absolutely unused, still carefully folded together, and spoiled, the way precious silks are spoiled when not used?"

And so the saint is one who lives life to the hilt. We are not saints because we are afraid of our own weaknesses and of the difficulties of life. Instead of giving ourselves enthusiastically to life, we approach it half-heartedly. By impoverishing the life of the spirit, we heighten the temptation of the world, the flesh, and the devil. As St. Thomas says: "No man can live without

delight, and that is why a man deprived of spiritual joy
goes over to carnal pleasures."

We do not begin to live once we have solved our
problems. We solve our problems by living. That is what
our Lord meant when He spoke of losing your life in order
to save it: in other words, do not try to save it by guarding and hoarding it carefully, fretfully, but by living it,
spending it rightfully, bravely, unstintingly.

Since the full human life consists essentially in progressive knowledge and love of God, the practical question is: How do we grow in the loving awareness of God?
The first way is by listening to His word. His word
reached its most trenchant power and shimmering
clarity in the embodiment of Christ. The best way, therefore, to come to know God is by knowing Christ, Who is
God in His most attractive form, so infinitely attractive,
in fact, that it is impossible to know Him without loving
Him. The most important question ever asked in the
history of the world was the question our Lord asked at
Caesaria Philippi when He asked: "What think ye of
Christ?" And the men He asked, who were the leaders
and scholars of that day, were unable to answer because they had never learned to listen receptively,
openly, and so they never came to know by experience
the reality of God in their midst.

So the scriptural movement as it exists today is a
good beginning toward this experiential encounter with
the real Christ, but it must become more than a studious
effort or a scientific investigation. The Bible Vigil,
fortunately, is becoming more and more popular and is
certainly one of the most effective ways of setting the
stage for a concrete, personal I-Thou relationship between God and man.

A second way of growing in the loving awareness of

God and thus becoming truly human is by looking intently upon the real, unfabricated image of Christ. This real and unfabricated image of Christ is preserved for us and kept alive in the liturgy. Religion, then, must announce; it must prepare the way for the sacred IMAGE OF CHRIST which speaks to the believer out of the memory of the Church.

We have no document which speaks of Jesus purely from the viewpoint of history. And if we did, it would have no more relevance or value than a photograph. The portrait we do have of Christ is based on a faithful, accurate reminiscence, a reminiscence fathered by the Holy Spirit. This inspired memory of the Church attains the Son of God in reality, with eyes capable of seeing the Lord and a mind capable of understanding His message. The image of Christ took shape in the reminiscence of an Apostle as such, invested with the role of laying bare the portrait of the Lord. This Apostle—Matthew, for instance—was not a private individual but a bishop of the Church. It was in virtue of the authority which he possessed in the Church that he evoked his memories and proclaimed them. And so it is precisely the memory of the Bridegroom, of the Church, that provides for us the only reliable portrait of Christ. Even the Gospels are just a part—an extremely important part—of the memory of the Church.

This true image is a living thing with its immutable core in the Incarnation and Redemption; but its character changes. Even among the Evangelists there are differences of nuance and tone. But all of them give us one objective Christ, the unique embodiment of God, to contemplate.

Christ Himself, then, is the Mystery which is seen by angels, and "believed in the world." Yet Christ has been seen in the world too, and therefore faith is not incompatible with every form of "sight." Does the Ascension of Christ into glory mean that men have been deprived of this epiphany, this "shining forth of God"? The Church assures us that this is not so, for not only has Christ our God been seen from Christmas to Ascension by thousands of men whose bodies have gone to the dust long ago, but He is seen today: "Visibly we see God," says the Christmas Preface. So there is something even now to rejoice our hearts. Where can we see Him? In the "breaking of bread," as did the disciples of Emmaus. St. Leo said: "What was visible in our Redeemer has now passed into mysteries."

To repeat and sum up this capital point about the structure of religion: The Word was made flesh, thus becoming for us the absolute Image of God. Christ is the Sign of God, and it is because He signifies God in a visible, tangible way. He is no less seen and no less known by men in the twentieth century than by the disciples of the first. This is why the liturgical movement should not overlook or play down the "memorial" aspect of the Eucharist. "Do this in memory of me," our Lord commanded. And so one of the vastly important things we do in the liturgy is reminisce about Christ. St. Teresa of Avila is often cited as an ardent exponent of the liturgy. But why she was such an enthusiast is not ordinarily added. It was precisely because the liturgy managed to focus her mind on the Lord. "All of our trouble comes," she said, "from not keeping our eyes on Him."

This whole idea, it seems to me, is summed up best and most succinctly by none other than J. D. Salinger when he says: "See Christ and you are a Christian; all else is talk."

Theological Mysticism

A man cannot become perfectly human until he becomes partly divine. This divinizing process is the mystical life.

A man cannot understand Scripture unless he first, at least inchoately, understands Christ. Remember what St. Paul said in 2 Corinthians 3:15–16: "To this day, I say, when the law of Moses is read out, a veil hangs over their hearts. There must be a turning to the Lord first, and then the veil will be taken away." And no man knows Christ "unless it is a gift from the Father." (John 6:66)

And this disclosure on the part of Christ is a mystical experience. No man follows unless drawn. Bonaventure defines faith as "that habit of the mind whereby we are drawn and captivated into the following of Christ." Any life lived by deep faith is necessarily a mystical life. The apostolic tradition began with a mystical experience. Remember when those rugged, untutored fishermen tried to get Christ to explain Who He was and what He was about? He simply said: "Come and see." And they went and saw and learned first hand by experience Who Christ was. Later on, John the Evangelist bases the whole Christian thing—fellowship between God and man—on this kind of mystical experience (1 John 1). When Christ prayed to His Father: "That they all may be one as Thou Father art in Me and I in Thee," He was praying for a world full of mystics.

Mystical experience may be defined as the experiential knowledge of the deep things of God or a suffering of diving things. The explanation cannot be sought in any rational intuition of God. God cannot be seen piecemeal. In mystical experience, God is known through *union of love*. It is the supernatural love of charity which alone can connaturalize the soul to Deity: this love becomes, according to the expression of John of St. Thomas, the objective means of knowledge. The soul suffers the touch of God Who makes grace fructify in love, and in this "suffering" which is still an effect of God but an effect at which the soul does not stop, God is experientially known; He is touched and tasted as immediately as possible, although still (and even more than ever) in night, in a light which is illumination, according to the words of the psalm.

Supernatural mystical experience is bound to no condition of nature, to no particular temperament, or particular education or religious denomination, not to any technique whatsoever. It is bound only to the Gospel way of life pushed to its ultimate consequences, and in particular to detachment from perfection itself.

The mystical experience, in its most universal intelligible characteristics, is the fruitive experience of *an* absolute. And this is possible in the natural order. Its term is the substantial *existence* of the soul (not the essence of the soul). It is not a question of seeing, but of experiencing, of tasting; and what is tasted, touched here as if it were naked, is the existence of the soul at the root of the powers which emerge from it, for the intelligence, in emanating from the substance of the soul, is informed by it as by an intelligible species.

Here at the infinite and inexhaustible ground of his being man is liberated from his self-conscious, separative ego and is put in touch with ultimate reality and gains kinship with all contingent reality, so that now and only now is he ready for universal, unlimited ecumenism.

As St. Augustine said: "God is the only reality and we are only real insofar as we are in His order and He in us." This means that Christianity will have been successful when, in this whole wide world, there is just one

Christ responding perfectly to His Father's love. And this is achieved only when men can say: "I live now not I but Christ lives in me." And that will not even begin to happen until we get people beyond the threshold activities of the Church. As E. Underhill put it: "Mysticism is the passionate longing of man for God, the unseen reality, loved, sought, and adored in Himself for Himself alone." It is a metaphysical thirst. A mystic is not a person who practices unusual forms of prayer, but a person whose life is ruled by this thirst. He is sensitive to and responds to the overwhelming attraction of God. This is not an invitation to religious emotionalism. It is a profound philosophical truth which is a theological truth, too (East and West).

The experience—first hand—of God may come in many ways and under many symbolic disguises. It may be steady or fleeting, dim or intense. But, insofar as it is direct and intuitive it is always a mystical experience. So, a first hand experience of God the Absolute Reality and a life controlled by the love which that experience awakens—this is what unites all mystics, Christian and non-Christian alike; therefore, unity of the human world depends upon the growing number of mystics.

This concept of mysticism relieves us from narrow and exclusive conceptions since God's demand on the human person, His confrontation with man—this man, personal, unique, unrepeatable—is a universal truth experienced by different people in many different ways and degrees. This statement seems to cover all mystics—from the impersonal ecstasy of the pagan Plotinus, with his longing after the one, to the Christocentric passion of St. Bernard or Richard Rolle, from the eucharistic mysticism of St. Thomas or Catherine of Genoa to the inner light of the Quaker saints. It is part of the business of organized religion to arouse and feed this Godward thirst and so to make us more human, more alive.

This God-centered vitality makes a man not only alive to God but alive to God's world, delicately and intelligently in tune with what goes on there. This worldly-grounded theology, so characteristic of religion in the Western world, is due to the predominance of the Incarnation principle, namely, that man becomes, at his full development a creative personality, a tool of God. The promise made in the first chapter of Acts is literally fulfilled in Him: His living contemplation of the eternal, His prayer in the Spirit, produces power, power on earth.

As a consequence of this unfolding principle, all of our genuine mystics turn out to be earthy mystics, not content with self-loss in peace and blessedness of eternity. For the earthy mystic, union with God means self-giving to the purposes of Divine energy and love in the world. And so, St. Paul, St. Bernard, St. Francis, St. Joan of Arc, John Wesley, Elizabeth Fry, and the Curé of Ars lived lives of immense apostolic power and agreed with Ruysbroeck's saying that the final stage of the mystic is not ecstatic self-loss in the Godhead but something at once more difficult and divine—"a wide-spreading love toward all in common." This is what Baron von Hügel calls "inclusive mysticism," which precludes pantheistic tendencies and sloppy claims to be in tune with the Infinite.

TOWARDS AN ECUMENICAL SPIRITUALITY

by Frank van het Hof *

WE LEAVE the dark history of our oppositions to turn together toward a new future. The worth of present-day Christians will be shown in the relinquishment of their confessional warfare, "in not trying to find out who was wrong and who was right" as Pope John expressed it. That does not imply minimizing the importance of truth and the affirmation of basic doctrinal positions. But if these real problems were the only thing dividing us we would be nearer than we suppose. This can never be stressed enough. If there is one certain truth of the gospel which cannot possibly be denied, it is indeed this unity between those who confess the name of Christ.

Ecumenism as a Way of Life

A flame has been enkindled for unity all over the world. We must try to make it more alive, more radiating, by meeting for ecumenical prayer and for ecumenical work. *It is necessary to believe in the light during the*

* Frank van het Hof, Brother of Taize (a Protestant monastic group started after World War II), was born in the Netherlands in 1935. After a classical education, he went through teacher training at Nijmegen. He was pursuing university classical language study when, in 1960, he became a member of the Taiz community. He has published articles in France and Holland.

night and force the dawn to arrive. This time especially, we are looking from midst of darkness at "the lamp shining in a murky place, until the day breaks and the morning star rises to illuminate our minds" (2 Peter 1:19). A Christian always looks forward. Again and again we must try to realize this principle of life more fully. Our eyes, our interior attitude, our whole life must be turned to the future. *A Christian does not look back, even at the day just past.* It is as with a plant. "A plant which is not turned towards the light withers. In the same way a Christian who refuses to look at the light of God but on the contrary wants to see nothing but the shadows is condemned to a slow death. He cannot grow and build himself up in Christ." [1] We must wish to turn ourselves towards the light.

That means that we need some lines of action, some principles for an ecumenical attitude, that can lead us during the whole year. Ecumenism is not an abstract doctrine, an ideology among others; an ecumenical Christian tries to make of ecumenism a *way of life.* Ecumenism is not only the concern of the hierarchy, the church-leaders, the theologians and some people that found in it new spiritual teddy bears. Ecumenism concerns every Christian. "De Oecumenismo", the *Decree on Ecumenism* adopted by the Fathers at the Vatican Council says it very clearly and gives certain directions for Catholic Christians.

How can each Christian at each moment respond personally to the ecumenical vocation, to this call for renewal? For renewal of the Church and Ecumenism can not be separated. And this renewal too, *this aggiornamento,* concerns every Christian man and Christian woman, old and young. The *aggiornamento* of the

1. Roger Schutz, *Unity Man's Tomorrow* (London: The Faith Press, 1962), p. 93.

Church demands the *aggiornamento* of every member personally. The reform of exterior structures can not succeed if there is not at the same time a reform of our selves, of our lives, a conversion of our mentalities, a change of our hearts. *"There can be no ecumenism worthy of the name without a change of heart,"* states the Decree on Ecumenism. This call for *aggiornamento* is a *challenge* for the Christian life of everyone of us. *"Every renewal of the Church is essentially grounded in an increase of fidelity to her own calling. Undoubtedly this is the basis of the movement toward unity."* The faithful should remember that the more effort they make to live holier lives according to the Gospel, the better will they further Christian unity and put it into practice. For the closer their union with the Father, the Word and the Spirit, the more deeply and easily will they be able to grow in mutual brotherly love. This change of heart and holiness of life, along with public and private prayer for the unity of Christians, should be regarded as the soul of the whole ecumenical movement and merits the name *"spiritual ecumenism."*

I should like to share with you some principles of spiritual life in ecumenical perspective, some principles of an *ecumenical spirituality* as we try to live these in Taizé, the Protestant monastic community in France. Our Rule proposes to every Brother of the Community (we are sixty-six now of different Protestant confessions and different nations) *"to be consumed with burning zeal for the unity of the Body of Christ."* How can he personally reply to that vocation? By feeding the flame which has been lighted for unity throughout the world. In staying before God alone or in common prayer; kneeling, standing, sitting—it does not matter! We know, that unity is God's supernatural work, and that all our action has only some value in so far as it continues that prayer and makes it become true.

"To keep ourselves in God's presence is not beyond our strength, does not exceed our human capacity. We can do this even if we are not conscious of any feeling of God's presence, and even in times of loss of fervor, remembering that the objective presence of God does not depend on our awareness of it. Some people, having gone along this way a long time, will one day perhaps take a new step forward and make an offering of their life to God for the sake of unity." [2]

Prayer for Christian Unity

Here we have the first principle of an *ecumenical spirituality: prayer day after day with a burning zeal for the unity of the Body of Christ.* In speaking of prayer for the unity of Christians, we first must recall that it is no different from ordinary Christian prayer and is thus necessarily and indissolubly bound up, as all prayer is, with humility. We are not really praying unless we have this attitude of humility, this spirit of poverty which looks to God for everything. Prayer for this unity of Christians involves the other elements of Christian prayer as well: *adoration, confession of sins, thanksgiving and intercession.*

Adoration of God, Father, Son and Holy Spirit, perfectly one in three Persons. Christ, when he prayed for unity (John 17), asked for his Church and for his disciples the unity which binds him to the Father. Our prayer for the visible unity of Christians begins with the contemplation of this unity of God in three Persons. We shall contemplate as well God the Creator, the God who by his omnipotence, in his immensity, holds the entire

2. *Ibid.,* p. 85.

creation together, by his governance causing the unity of the universe—the unity which, having been disturbed by man's sin, has been restored by Christ's sacrifice. Christ died for all men. Contemplation of the Spirit directs our attention to the Lord who desires to be everywhere, to penetrate everything, in order to bring everything towards the perfect unity of his kingdom. The Christian, a living member of a truly universal Church, prays for this inclusive unity which will embrace all men: for the Church does not consider itself some kind of closed society, a club for the privileged.

Confession of sins also plays its part in the prayer for unity. Prayer for unity cannot be valid if it is not an act of *humility* wherein man confesses his responsibility in the division. This confession of sins commits us to real repentance, *a new conversion,* to a real change in our lives. Our prayer for unity leads us to a better obedience to Christ, to a life of faith in a charity which believes all things, hopes all things, and bears all things.

Our prayer for Unity is also one of thanksgiving, thanksgiving for the concern we have today over lost unity, for the apostles of unity, for men like Pope John, for Abbé Couturier, a great apostle of unity in France, who died some years ago.

Our prayer is also intercession, supplication. Bring before God the needs of divided Christians, pray for each other, for the needs of the world, for a new Pentecost of the Church. Our *intercession* is in a way a sharing of our difficulties and our sufferings—a sharing that takes place in the presence of God as an appeal to Him to heal this wound of our division.[3] It is *waiting for God,* for the event of God in our lives, in the life of the Church, in the life of the world. For us, Brothers of Taizé, this *contemplative*

---

3. Cf. Max Thurian, *Visible Unity and Tradition* (Baltimore: Helicon Press, 1962).

expectation of the event of God, of the unity, is our first vocation.

Peace

This prayer can be made in private and in community. The *Christian community*—and among these the monastic type community—is the melting-pot of the ecumenical spirit, the place where we discover and where we learn the necessity of an *irenicism* which goes as far as possible. It is a place where we learn to make peace within ourselves, to eliminate all violence and aggressiveness in us before we are able to communicate this peace to others.

"Because Christ has reconciled us, we in our turn have to reconcile all men. And because Christ has forgiven us we must in turn forgive: Forgive us—as we also forgive." This is a totally new fact in human history: reconciled by Christ, forgiven, clothed in peace, men can now live together in a single body, in the Church.

> The peace of reconciliation restores the unity that had been lost and frees man from his natural distress. Divided within himself, man wants to do the good which he loves but nevertheless does the evil which he hates. To this divided man is addressed an appeal—to live in the peace of Christ, the source of unity: "may the peace of Christ, into which you have been called in order to form one body reign in your hearts;" which means in the deepest part of ourselves—in the most secret depths of our personalities.
>
> The peace of Christ dwells in us every time we reconcile ourselves with our neighbor. However, if we are not reconciled how can we approach God, how can we approach his altar? . . . This peace of Christ dwells in us every time we are instruments of reconciling our neighbor with God—by forgiveness, by compassion, by tenderness of heart.[4]

4. Schutz, *Unity*, pp. 68–69.

"Ambrose of Milan tells us: 'Begin the work of peace with yourself so that once at peace we can bring peace to the others'. So that I can be a peace-bearer a conversion of attitudes needs to take place in me. . . . My early upbringing has a hold on me, all the habits of life and thought which forms part of the depths of a man's personality, can be opposed to a real communion with my neighbor." [5] It is only when my sight is completely rectified that I shall see man before me not in the light of his lesser qualities but above all in the light of the very best that is in him. We have to meet our neighbor, our fellow Christian in the community, the Christian of another Church, in the light of Christ. We have to know that in every man, even in the man who does not confess Christ, there shines the reflection of the very image of the Creator. Our neighbor is not just the man whom we like but the man whom life has wounded and set at the side of our path. To look at a fellow Christian in this light is first of all to see in him a Christ-bearer.

It is therefore not exaggerated to say that being concerned with brotherly life in a Christian community means being a *worker for Christian unity*. Every Christian community must continue to make this unity, which already exists, ever deeper.

Unity of the Person

Unity among the members of a community presupposes that we agree on the prior necessity of each member being at one in himself. *This unity of the person is of greatest importance.* We must continually try to find this unity if we are to achieve and maintain this balance of the human person—try to coordinate our thinking and our action. For the Christian, the way to unity is by harmonizing his actions with the thought of Christ who

5. *Ibid.*, pp. 70–71.

lives within him, by living the faith he professes.

Every quest for unity among men implies first of all that a man who is engaged in it is careful to see that he has this unity in his own person. To reverse this order would be putting the cart before the horse. Just in so far as we can overcome *the disintegration that threatens us day by day by such inner unity of ourselves,* so it becomes possible to work for unity between men and to await eagerly the visible unity of all Christians in one Church.[6]

"Bless and Curse Not"

Just as for members of a monastic community there is the task of seeking unity within their own group, so for Christians who have received the vocation of marriage there is the obligation to live the vocation of unity first of all in their families, their households. Some Fathers of the Church called a household *"the little Church of God."* In recent years a movement for young couples, the so-called *"Households of unity"* has come into existence. These couples live the spirituality of Taizé. They make some commitments, for a year. They try to be in the midst of their own confessions, or else in the heart of human circles deafened to the Gospel, partly because of the inconsistency of our Christian separations, *a little lamp, a little sign of unity and hope.* Let me read you something of their *Rule of life.*

> The inward call toward Christian unity is renewed by the aspiration to fulfill the Gospel. Because of its demand of love towards all men, the Gospel cannot allow us to maintain an attitude of hostility toward certain Christian groups. This need to be consistent with the evangelical profession of love conceals an incalculable strength, able to be one of the instruments which will one day overthrow the confessional barriers.

6. Cf. *ibid.,* p. 16.

Those who adopt this stand do not intend to judge the Christians who went before them. They simply believe that, for themselves, a staunch determination is asked of them, for they can no longer help perpetuate Christian divisions. In a sense, they have become conscientious objectors in the face of the inconsistency of the divisions between Christians.

A Household of Unity commits itself to a common minimum:

a) To pray three times a day.

b) Each week to practice a "re-examination of life" between husband and wife.

c) To prepare with special care the Week of Prayer for Unity. This week must be the great opportunity for meetings at home.

d) To practice a very generous hospitality in order to manifest openness toward others. A Household of Unity invites guests at least once a week.

e) To keep only the requisite minimum of its material possessions. The earth belongs to the Lord. A Christian wishes the material goods to be distributed among all men.

Unity and Mission

The *Christian Community* is, as we saw, an important place for *ecumenical spirituality*. It is a question of *being before acting*. It is important to *live our Christian unity today,* in a spirit of peace, of love, with the outlook of Christ himself, in an attitude of humble prayer. *One does not argue about unity, one lives it.* Otherwise reasons—good reasons for or against—mount up.

Yes, there are the impossibilities, indeed. There are more than enough of them to discourage us. But a discouraged man—unable to keep the unity of the Spirit in the bond of peace—such a man cannot be a worker for Christian unity. And is not a Christian a man who is never discouraged because always forgiven?

But unity is not an end in itself: Christ did not only pray "that they may be ONE," but he went on to pray "that the world may believe," that is to say that by their unity the world may be given the possibility of believing.

To be ONE so that the world may believe! There are two steps here: *the first*—for us Christians to reunite; *the second*—for us to unite so that we can bring God to those who do not believe.

As we saw, ecumenical spirituality *embraces the whole of life.* Today, a great number of walls, built up between the different spheres of human existence, must be swept away. We cannot speak about prayer and ecumenical spirituality in an abstract way. It is the ecumenical spirituality of a concrete man in a modern civilization, of a man who is aware that a new world is coming, different from the actual one. We have to prepare ourselves for the confrontation with a new society and Christians have to banish fear of this new future. We cannot live in fear. The man who wants to work for unity, and with this in view wishes to become part of the coming civilization, must first of all shut out fear. *When a man's foundation is in God he has nothing to fear. He is sure of victory before he starts.*

If it is true that we can say in ecumenism *being before acting,* that does not mean, that acting has no importance. This *ecumenical spirituality* has to lead us into as many activities as possible, but always activities which are *a consequence* of our spiritual life, of our spiritual life, of our prayer, of our liturgical life, of our life in brotherly love. *A great dynamism has to push us forward,* building on our way *visible signs* that express our new mentality and our desire to live in unity with each other. Today *gestures* seems to be more effective than words. Especially the *young generation* wants to see visible progress, visible consequences of what we profess with our lips. In these signs we can express our *spirit of reconciliation.*

Three years ago in Taizé we started an *ecumenical collection:* OPERATION HOPE. The intention was that a Protestant community, Taizé, would help Catholic bishops and some Pentecostal parishes in Latin America with some very necessary reforms on the social level. This collection aroused a great interest in France. Let me give some examples. A Protestant and a Catholic parish in a large city had common services during lent and together offered the money to OPERATION HOPE. They lived together by prayer and by action the common vocation of Christians in the world, *that is, to cry a word of hope to mankind,* to live a life that in itself is a sign of hope, to build up *signs of hope* among those of our brothers who have lost all human hope. Another plan is now to distribute *one million New Testaments* in an ecumenical edition among poor Catholic and Protestant Christians of Latin America.

Much more can be said on this subject of *ecumenical spirituality.* Certainly we did not speak about all its aspects. Some people make a separation between *ecumenism of the intelligence* and *ecumenism of the heart.* However, there cannot be any opposition between these two ways. *Ecumenism of the intelligence* is ecumenism of prudent wisdom and vigilance. *Ecumenism of the heart* is ecumenism of imprudent audacity and of hope. The first speaks often of "exigencies," the second of mercy. The first one, in a realistic vision of insurmontable difficulties sits down before building the tower. The second, in a prophetic vision of the miracle, has the impatient expectation of the event of God and prays for its realization. These two aspects are complementary aspects of one ecumenical reality, on the level of the person and of the community.

In Taizé, there is an involvement in ecumenical work through the magazine *Verbum Caro,* an ecumenical magazine for theology, through books, ecumenical groups for dialogue, participation in the work of the World Council of Churches, presence at the Vatican Council and other activities. But first of all in our monastic vocation an accent is placed on the ecumenical ministry lived not on the level of ideas, but of faith, hope and charity, by means of communal prayer, brotherly love, and simple and meaningful gestures.

For us, in Taizé, it is impossible to separate the monastic vocation and the ecumenical vocation, since for every Christian ecumenism is part of his vocation of being a Christian, of being a member of the universal Church. And as a member of the Body of Christ, who has received by baptism the vocation of working for unity and reconciliation among men, we have to cry a word of hope to mankind by our words and our deeds. Love is a revolutionary force; mercy is greater than severity; the movement is away from the juridical to the personal— stressing above all the individual, personal encounter with Christ. He transfigures the shadows in us, about which sometimes we can do nothing, so that through a slow elaboration, what is still dark, restless, violent, is peacefully enlightened and taken up into God. Only gazing on Christ makes possible the slow transformation of ourselves and of the Church, of which we are the members. In gazing on Christ we become aware that we are among the poor of the earth. In gazing on Him we will discover that the "catholic" vocation means just this, as a French bishop, Mgr. Huyghe, bishop of Arras, said.

He is Catholic who opens himself to all, who lets resound in his heart the universal love of the Lord. He is Catholic who, in remembrance of the mercy of Christ for him, becomes merciful, that is to say, painfully and profoundly moved by misery, misery in all its forms. He is Catholic who instinctively rejects all that is a source of division, who cannot encounter another without seeking a ground of understanding with him. He is Catholic who sees in each man not the social category to which that man belongs, neither the label of non-believer, of Protestant, of Jew nor of Communist, but the Brother for whom Christ has died and who has been placed along his path to receive his love. Finally, he is Catholic, who creates in himself by humility a soul like that to be found in the poor and the miserable, and who is always ready to welcome all those who are deprived, be it of material goods, be it of the light of the faith.

ECUMENISM AND SPIRITUALITY

by Douglas Steere *

I HAVE accepted the invitation to this seminar because I believe that real ecumenical advance can only come about when the discussion leaves Rome or Geneva or the great conferences and comes into every walk of life. And to have it penetrate into the seminaries and universities and become a part of the approach which is made there to every subject is a most heartening step forward.

I must confess that I was intrigued by your subject and by your daring at this stage of our inquiry to apply the ecumenical approach to the whole field of spirituality. For there are many who would shield with their lives this side of the Church's life from intrusion and who would feel that this is an area that will be the last to yield to an ecumenical approach because it is so intimately bound up with the very heart experiences of each form of religion, and therefore would defend itself to the last against change and against any intermingling with

* Douglas V. Steere (Quaker) is emeritus professor of philosophy at Haverford College. He received a B.S. in agriculture from Michigan State University, an M.A. and Ph.D. from Harvard and a B.A. and M.A. from Oxford. His books include *Prayer and Worship* (1938), *Work and Contemplation* (1957), and *Spiritual Counsels and Letters of Baron von Hügel* (1964).

the spiritual disciplines or experiences of another form of the Christian religion.

I have had no clue as to how others were to handle this subject and therefore what I do will have to be a very personal exploration and one that may be much on the surface and perhaps repeat much that you have already covered. Perhaps this in inevitable when you are breaking new ground, and perhaps, too, it may be particularly valuable if it should turn out that persons working in this area without any pre-arrangements should discover that they had a huge overlap of agreement and that they were nearer to each other than they could have believed. At any rate, I shall have to walk round this vast subject in my own way and share a few reflections on it that come to me, without any notion that this paper can be more than a preface to a preface.

I think that I would have to begin by noting that, for me, the notion that spirituality is such an inner citadel of the whole temple of a religion that it must be treated as a holy of holies and protected against all foreign eyes is not a congenial standpoint. If these foreign eyes are the eyes of men and women who are sincere seekers after God, as I think we must presuppose our brothers are in any serious ecumenical inquiry, then far from being walled out by the inner core of spirituality, I suspect that if it is a genuine spirituality, it will approach them with the assumption that they too stand in it already and that by more fully disclosing its heart center, they will find in it what they have long been seeking.

It is for me an interesting observation that the inwardly kindled, the Christian mystics have been the ones who have broken through all kinds of barriers and shown to those of other religious approaches the concern that they have for them and the love they have to share their vision with them. It is as if all of the tribal in the religion was brushed aside and this ecumenical world-embracing love at the core of the religion streamed forth in these persons. They seem free of that anxiety that makes tribal religion so tight and protective. When in the novel *Apartment in Athens*, the visitor speaking to the widow about her martyred husband says, "Your man Nicholas seemed to have none whatever of the self-preservative in him," she is describing what characterizes these mystically minded spirits who long to share what they have found and the self-preservative instinct of their religious approach recedes and its passion for souls pours forth. One thinks of an Origen or of a Francis of Assisi in the Nile Delta before the Sultan, or of a Raymond Lull dying at the hands of the Saracens to whom he had come to bring a message of Christ's love, or of a Nicholas of Cusa reaching out so far to the Muslims because he was himself so close to the center that he could be very free at the perifery, or of the Quaker John Woolman who regarded his Catholic brothers as of the one faith that he knew through the Quaker form, or of John XXIII with his boundless passion for showing how much God cares for all men. The story of John preaching in a Roman prison on the grace and mercy of God and being met afterwards by a murderer who asked him whether he felt that such mercy and grace could reach *even* to him, and of John's saying nothing but pulling him to his bosom is almost a symbol of the ecumenical outreach of the mystically minded who have felt the fire of God's love at the core of their being and know it to burn in all men and that they must answer to it beyond all barriers.

I think therefore that the first observation that we might make is that genuine Christian spirituality is always breaking bonds and crossing boundaries often to the embarrassment of the more cautious custodians of religion and that these souls have a way of recognizing each other across bounds and are therefore forerunners of the ecumenical spirit and perhaps are the ones who can be most relied upon to press forward its spirit. There could even be a strong case made for the fact that until there is a spiritual renewal and deepening, there is likely to be little more than legalistic ecumenism or one that is heavily infected with the secular passion for universalism which marks our time and which is little more than a leveling Leviathan that will not advance any of the re- ligions affected. There is certainly in any ecumenical movement a place for the institutional specialist who will help both in demolition and rebuilding. But unless these architects and construction firms are under the firm guidance of spiritually illuminated men and unless this has come out of inner vision and of an inner com- pulsion that does not derive from fear but from love and caring for the others that has been poured into their hearts by the passionate love of God, the outcome has little to commend it.

The second observation on ecumenism and spirituality is to look more closely at the way in which the character- istic spirituality of any religious group has been born, how it has been shaped, and what we may have a right to expect of it. For unless we are able to understand the process of the building up of these spiritual traditions, we are not likely to be able to learn from each other and we are not able to see that these traditions are them- selves subject to change—often to the most drastic change—and therefore that none of them are ever more than residues, precious as there may be, of the visitation of the spirit and that they dare not be canonized too finally lest God choose to break through in some utterly fresh way and we deny him entrance.

If I were to take one primary source of spirituality in

Roman Catholicism, in order to apply this kind of scrutiny to it, I might choose to examine its corporate ascetic experiences. Back of them lay the hard saying of Jesus and the ascetic practices that grew up both within the early Church and in groups like the Montanists in the second century of the Church. The martyrs and their ready self-abandonment played their part and there may even be some ground for believing that Eastern traditions of self-denial may also have entered in. But in the case of most of the monastic orders that grew out of the initial flight to the desert in Egypt and the East and that came later, there was an intensely personal need and an intensely personal decision and yielding, out of which a movement grew and spiritual practices were fashioned. It is interesting to note if one leaps from Pachomius and Basil to Benedict how much the particular social and political crisis of the time contributed to the context into which this form of spiritual association was fitted. There are able scholars of this whole movement who make a strong case for the fact that every monastic order with its own form of spirituality grew out of some man's total response to God in a crisis situation and was, in a way, God's peculiar answer to that situation, and that the order that may have grown out of the response of such a man was also implicit in this man's peculiar response. If this thesis is even partially sound, one could say without exaggerating that every one of the many monastic forms of spirituality bears the marks of the situation to which it was meant to speak, as well as to carry certain universal traits that mark all sound spirituality in any period.

If this is true, we might ask how Ignatian spirituality, which, while not monastic, is so fiercely devoted to disciplining the will and to producing totally obedient soldiers of Jesus Christ and of the Roman Catholic Church, grew out of the necessities of the Church in the sixteenth

century. And we might ask whether its self-conscious in-
dividualizing and shaping of all of the psychological
powers of men, using every known device, or the
familial conception of the Benedictines with its more
feudal family pattern and its notion that one is saved
through membership in the family of God and not by any
efforts at private devotion is any better adapted to meet
our needs. The little skit called *Brother Petroc's Return*
dramatizes some of these questions with striking charm.

When it is realized how heavily these historically fo-
cused orders have shaped even the spiritual patterns of
our laymen's retreats, which are often little more than
abbreviated forms of the initial *Spiritual Exercises* of
Ignatius of Loyola and have fashioned the norms of lay
piety, the responsibility for re-examining them with the
most penetrating queries as to their validity today becomes evident. Now in doing this in an ecumenical setting there is likely to be far less inclination to shy away
from some area because it is regarded as too sacred to
meddle with or even to scrutinize with full frankness.
When it is realized too that the spirituality of the Roman
Catholic Church has been so deeply shaped by monastic
piety and that it has often been almost identified with it,
the joint examination of the treasures of Roman Catholic
spirituality might promote an even greater desire to try
to put freshly to the fore the role of the lay apostolate
in a way that would see it in quite a different light than
as a member of an inferior third order or as a remotely
attached oblate.

It is an interesting feature of the growth of these monastic communities which were created often by laymen
and with their distinctive types of spirituality, that in the
beginning, the Roman Catholic Church had distinct reservations about their legitimacy and that again and
again there were deep suspicions of the semi-autono-

mous character which they seemed to exhibit and of whether they could be absorbed into the Church's life without severe danger. The fact that the Church was able to adopt these bodies and could incorporate them and put them to work for its life was one of the great acts of genius of the Church and is one that is worthy of study by ecumenists. For there is a sense that in holding all of these diverse orders together, the Church itself indicated that it had managed a considerable ecumenical task all along.

When the late Gustav Weigel remarked humorously at the Harvard ecumenical gathering in 1964 that if this ecumenical business went much further, even the Jesuits might be pressed into joining the Roman Catholic Church, there was more than a seed of humor in this suggestion. To put the matter in another way, these monastic corporate orders sprang up within the broad life the Church through the instrumentality of individuals and each bore the stamp both of the historical epoch and of the crisis out of which the person made this fresh response to God, and of the founder himself as well as exhibiting the characteristic marks of all spiritual experience and commitment. The Roman Catholic Church has therefore in its great treasury of monastic and institutional spirituality, a vast variety of historically and personally stamped responses to God, and when they are individually examined, this historical and personal source as well as the divine life that called them forth must be borne in mind or they often tend to assume a sacrosanct character that quite obscures their true nature.

A third observation about this subject of ecumenism and spirituality and one which will call for a great deal of careful work in the next period will be a probing into the issue of comparative spiritual practices in the Roman Catholic and non-Catholic communions. I will not mention the kind of probing that is involved in comparative studies of the liturgy, for that has already been extensively examined. I will try rather to cite the other areas where the spirituality within the two groups has been less subjected to study. Certainly, the Roman Catholic scholars have been far more active in making available a wider knowledge of their spiritual practices than have the Protestant group. And it may not be unimportant to suggest that Protestants, by and large, have had a certain suspicion of spiritual practices, being influenced by their early critical attacks on Roman Catholic "works" which they insisted were human means of acquiring merit and therefore in Protestant eyes detracting from the realization that only in God's grace and in the bestowal of that grace in Jesus Christ is there any merit at all and that all of these other devices are therefore to be suspect.

At the outset, it may be interesting to examine the observation that Catholic devotional practices are more likely to be more intimately and integrally connected with their liturgical worship and with the corporate practices of the Church than are Protestant practices. When a Roman Catholic retreat is held, it is more likely to be built around an exposition or a deeper understanding of the Mass or of Confession or other sacramental practices than would a similar Protestant retreat. Practices like the use of the Rosary and of the prayers connected with it again have been more integrated with corporate worship than have the instructions for private prayer in the Protestant Churches.

A good deal of work needs to be done to get adequate expositions of Protestant spiritual practices such as the use of hymns both at home and in the churches; the use of house worship and family worship; the practice of Bible reading in the home; the whole character of private prayer in the life of a Protestant and the elements which it accents; the kind of devotional reading other than the Bible which Protestants are drawn to use in daily worship; the role of witnessing and of spontaneous public prayer in the more informal midweek meetings which still characterize many Protestant groups; the creation of spiritual literature in Protestantism; the place of ascetic practices such as abstention from alcohol and tobacco or of excessive personal adornment with jewelry and the like and the practice of simplicity of living on the part of many of these groups. Each Protestant group has certain accents that mark it out and has produced hymns or poetry or spiritual journals or personal testimonies and saints that have embodied them to which it is of real importance to gain access if we expect that in such an ecumenical period as ours we shall be able to share deeply across the lines of difference.

The Anglican Church in the seventeenth Century had an exceptionally rich outflowering of poetry and devotional concern. The hymns of early Methodism, as of the Lutheran beginnings, are a treasure house of spirituality, as is Johann Sebastian Bach and his contribution. The Quaker journals of the first century of its existence as a movement are among the most moving of religious documents and the German-language books of devotion of the seventeenth and eighteenth century Pietists who populated this country in the latter part of that period are full of riches, which need translating and sharing. All of these things are marked by their historical and their personal situation as well as by the universal elements of spirituality which they contain and need to be studied precisely in the same way that it was suggested above that Catholic monastic and Jesuit spirituality should be scrutinized.

While I am sceptical about the attempt of a contemporary Anglican theologian named Thornton to try to distinguish a unique Anglican spirituality and to make it a form which accents the life in the world and in the midst of family, business and professional responsibility and a type which does not disparage the full use of the intellectual and rational powers of the person, it is certainly true that Protestant spirituality has been profoundly influenced by the stance in the world of the Protestant layman. It will be fascinating in the future if we carry through this comparative ecumenical enterprise to compare certain Protestant manuals with, say, Francis de Sales' *Introduction to the Devout Life* or Chautard's *Soul of the Apostolate* and see where the elements of common practice are to be found and where they differ both in detail and in tone.

The fourth observation is closely related to and presupposes the third, for when we have made these careful examinations of each other's devotional practices, then comes the matter of whether we will be able on the one hand to learn from each other, and on the other, whether we shall be in a position to develop an even deeper and more effective set of devotional practices than either possessed that might come to fruition out of this ecumenical clasping of each others' life in our common longing to make a deeper response to God's compassionate love.

It is interesting to look back and to see what an impetus was given to this learning from each other by the tragic circumstances of the Hitler period in Germany. Because Roman Catholics knew that their people would have to stand alone before many agonizing personal moral decisions, they longed for them to have the strength of Bible-reading to support them and hundreds of thousands of copies of the New Testament were placed in the hands of Roman Catholic laity in that period. On the Protestant side, when their sermons were being monitored by secret informers or officials, they began to discover the power and strength of a liturgy that was not based so heavily on the contemporary word of the preacher and to introduce "high church" practices.

After the war the German Evangelical Academies that sprang up all over Germany were not unlike the facilities of the monasteries of the Catholic Church which had long been used to quicken the laity by retreats and instruction that were given there. Yet the stimulus of the consultations with the laity and the listening to the laity which these Protestant academies practiced produced several Catholic attempts in the same direction which may do much to cross these traditions.

In the matter of retreats, there is a considerable movement in Protestantism to discover how to use these vehicles effectively in the context of Protestant spirituality. Some of this is quite old in bodies like the Anglicans whose Anglo-Catholic renewal in 1833 tended especially to favor this device. Non-Anglican bodies have made far greater deviations from Roman Catholic practice in conducting their retreats than have the Anglicans and these groups keenly welcome the chance for an interchange of experience and of practice and experiment within the wider ecumenical context.

Roman Catholic practice with various types of third orders and confraternities is of real interest to Protestant spiritual guides whose fellowship groups and guilds have had erratic results that would indicate the need for deeper understanding of what they are about.

On the side of such spiritual exercises as witnessing and stewardship or generous giving to those in need as a spiritual exercise, there are areas where we need close consultation.

While the greatest hope of authentic spiritual renewal

seldom comes from external need, there is no denying that it can be accentuated by such need and often some great spirit called out to speak to that need. If we face this situation frankly, it is more than clear that both Catholic and Protestant face the common element of scientism and secularism and general affluence in this technological age and that in the face of this, they must acknowledge the feebleness and even the irrelevancy of much that is pressed on their people as spirituality in our time. Both Protestant and Roman Catholic have not made up their minds about modern psychiatry and its claims, but both, because of their own lack of spiritual power, are inclined to turn parishioners over to these "secular priests" of our period and to use them as the last hospice for troubled situations. There was a time when they were themselves the last hospice and when society looked to them to find a spiritual resolution to these problems. Certainly there are medical cases in abundance for which this is a legitimate turnover. But quite as certainly there are a vast number of borderline cases where if our spirituality were deep enough and valid enough, we might give help to these persons from within the Christian community. One of the fascinating and almost unexplored areas of the use of what the spiritual director might learn from modern depth psychology would be to see what could be done with these tools of counselling to help persons move from a mediocre social and spiritual adjustment into one of deep inner commitment and an opening of themselves to spiritual power of a magnitude that few dream of today. This may be a field in which both Catholic and Protestant in a common quest may have an enormous amount to give to each other.

The lack of any place for the life of contemplation in modern society and the frantic flight from themselves which one sees in the retired group of men and women of advanced age today is a condition of common concern to both Catholic and Protestant, for both suffer deeply from its grim results and it dries up the springs of spiritual response in the members of both bodies. At a time when the technological revolution and automation are offering vast new areas of leisure across the board to people of all life stations, there is a cloud of fear of being alone and of using this leisure to deepen their relationship with God and their fellows. It is most heartening to see Father MacNamara and his Carmelite Spiritual Institute developing what he calls *Houses of Leisure and Learning* with facilities for prayer and for reading and consultation and with some person having some contemplative gifts as a resident in each house. These are not monasteries in the religious sense but rather are places of refuge in the world and for people of the world whether they are Catholic, Protestant, or of no acknowledged faith at all. Here is an area where we both need to work and where we could, if we had an ecumenical approach, be an enormous support to each other.

None of us know how to move forward in this area. None of us know fully how to break through to the deeper levels in order to make a layman who is prepared in private for life in the world and who can bring what he has found in the life of the world back into touch with its ground. None of us really know how to share the enormous power reserve of intercessory prayer with the laity of our generation so that they may take it up and use it for the redeeming of our time. None of us know fully how to counter the incredible power of the dispersive extrovert forces of our time in order to produce God-centered interior men who can live in the world and help both to carry it and to guide it into becoming a more compassionate society.

Now I am not suggesting that any Ecumenical Com-

mittee on the Deepening of the Spiritual Life of Our
Time is likely to accomplish any of these things. They
will be done in God's good Providence and be stirred by
His Holy Spirit. But I am suggesting that there are ob-
stacles which exist now to preparing the way for such a
movement which would not exist in the same way if we
as Catholics and Protestants were able to pool our resources and to meet each other in brooding over these
common problems in an atmosphere of trust and confidence. This confidence does not yet exist. There is still
a suspicion that one or the other will use these ecumenical liberties for their particular advantage. There is
still a deep suspicion in a wide range of the Protestant
spectrum that theologically the Roman Catholic approach to spirituality is Pelagian and therefore not to be
trusted or encouraged and that we can never make common cause with it. On the Roman Catholic side there is
a sense of unconscious superiority—and at times it may
even not confine itself to the unconscious level—and of
over-confidence in having been the custodian of these
vast spiritual treasures in the past and of doubt that
Protestant corporate worship is valid enough and rich
enough to support any structure of spiritual practice for
individual persons that might be built around it. We
have so much to overcome in the way of confidence and
in the way of these major accents which have so long
been associated with each of us that they cling to us
even when it can be shown that both of us have Pelagian and both of us have Augustinian elements and
that both of us need to move into an area of response to
grace that will make light of either tendency and see
that there is a time for letting go and a time for hang-
ing on.

If John V. Taylor, leading missionary statesman of the
Anglican Church, is right that "it is anxiety more than

any other factor which keeps separated Christians apart"
and that a divided Church approaching a reluctant and
elusive world is like trying "to catch a shoal of herring
with fifty shrimping nets" and that "History is the time
of God's patience, it is the space which he gives us in
which to obey his imperative," then in this area of spirituality, my prayer is that we may try that patience no
longer and surge forward into that common area of
search which he has long ago commanded us to enter.

SPIRITUALITY IS FOR ANGELS—
THE ANGELS OF MICHAEL

by Robert Bertram *

SEPTEMBER 29 was Michaelmas or, as some of us know it, the Feast of Saint Michael and All Angels. For a saint's day this one enjoys an unusually ecumenical popularity—"throughout the church," says one authority sweepingly.[1] The festival's ecumenicity and especially its feting of the angelic spirits make it a fit occasion for the theme of this seminar, Ecumenism and Spirituality. I propose to exploit this historic (if arbitrary) coincidence.

"Propose" is the right word. For in what follows I should like to venture not a documentary on how much "ecumenism and spirituality" are going on statistically and organizationally but rather a theological proposal of what, on the strength of our common biblical and churchly heritage, we dare to *believe* is going on. This proposal is itself, I suppose, a venture in ecumenism and spirituality—the riskiest kind. However, I should not

* Robert W. Bertram (Lutheran), Associate Professor of Systematic and Historical Theology at Concordia Seminary in St. Louis, did advanced study in Catholic theology at the University of Munich (1965–66). His publications include editing *Theology in the Life of the Church* (Fortress, 1963).

1. F. L. Cross (editor), *The Oxford Dictionary of the Christian Church* (London: Oxford University Press, 1957), p. 897.

pretend that the faith here expressed has no basis in churchly fact. Faith has eyes to see, and what it sees is in fact, already and very visibly, a flourishing spirituality of the most ecumenical sort. While, as you would expect, I speak as a confessing Lutheran—that is, confessing the gospel as it comes to the church's Lutherans—I trust that the host of witnesses I invoke, both in footnotes and text, is ecumenical enough to allow, for example, for even a very singular exegesis of the name "Michael" and for a singularly militant and mundane concept of "spirituality."

The kind of spirituality, however, to which this seminar is dedicated may seem at first to have little in common with the kind of spirits who come to mind on Michaelmas. Offhand, so it would seem. And that initial misgiving seems only to worsen when we see the scriptural text which traditionally is appointed as the epistle lesson for this festival, Revelation 12:7–12.

> Now war arose in heaven, Michael and his angels fighting against the dragon; and the dragon and his angels fought, but they were defeated and there was no longer any place for them in heaven. And the great dragon was thrown down, that ancient serpent, who is called the Devil and Satan, the deceiver of the whole world—he was thrown down to the earth, and his angels were thrown down with him. And I heard a loud voice in heaven, saying, "Now the salvation and the power and the kingdom of our God and the authority of his Christ have come, for the accuser of our brethren has been thrown down, who accuses them day and night before our God. And they have conquered him by the blood of the Lamb and by the word of their testimony, for they loved not their lives even unto death. Rejoice then, O heaven and you that dwell therein! But woe to you, O earth and sea, for the devil has come down to you in great wrath, because he knows that his time is short!" (RSV)

Michael and His Angels

This text, initial appearances to the contrary notwithstanding, does have something to say to the matter at hand, ecumenism and spirituality. It does, because it has something to say to that common sin which jeopardizes both ecumenism and spirituality, the sin of worldliness, though I regret having to dignify the sin with such a wonderfully earthy, world-affirming term. It is the sin, let us say, of a spurious and demonic secularism, the sin of capitulating not just to the world but to the world's tyrannical captor, "that ancient serpent, who is called the Devil and Satan, the deceiver of the whole world." Not that the text makes a case for *other*-worldliness, as if that were even the opposite of worldiness. Neither, by the way, does the text require us to prove the existence of angels. That, if nothing else, would be a discourtesy to the angels. Least of all do I want to plead for what Maritain in another connection brands as "angelism." [2] On the contrary, it is angelism precisely, that pseudo-spiritual abhorrence of things terrestrial, which I would argue Christian spirituality is not. And this text, for all its talk about angels and dragons and a war in heaven, for all of its "woe to you, O earth and sea," is mighty for just that argument. The spirituality which is most ecumenical is not a flight of the Alone to the Alone, or "what the individual does with his solitariness," [3] if that implies a retreat from the world's battles. Rather it is

2. Jacques Maritain, *Three Reformers: Luther, Descartes, Rousseau* (London: Sheed and Ward, 1950), p. 54. This theme reappears in Maritain's philosophy of art. See his *Art and Scholasticism*, tr. by J. F. Scanlan (London: Sheed and Ward, 1930), pp. 23, 78, 91, 135. I, like many others, cannot silence the wish that Maritain would retract his chapter on Luther in *Three Reformers*, a chapter so conspicuously unworthy of its distinguished author, just as in *Art and Scholasticism* (p. 60) he did see fit to retract his earlier criticism of Stravinsky.

3. Alfred North Whitehead, *Religion in the Making* (New York: Macmillan, 1926), p. 16.

from beginning to end, at least until the *Parousia,* a combat which resounds with the clash of arms, with "the sword of the Spirit," in the thick of the battle between Michael and his adversary. To that issue, which engages not only the Christian *oikumene* but the whole race and indeed the cosmos, this text does pertain, directly and vividly.

At first blush that may be a little hard to believe, for nothing could seem more irrelevant to our secular world today than this story about angels—unless, of course, we ourselves happened to *be* these angels. Which, as it turns out, we are. At least according to one durable exegetical tradition, (which includes such an anti-allegorizing exegete as Martin Luther) there is reason to suppose that the "angels" to whom Saint John here refers are not those celestial, disembodied spirits who are already gathered around the throne of grace but are rather those angels of God who are still on earth—in other words, you and I and all our fellow Christians.[4] "Sanctos homines," Augustine calls them.[5] These angels of Michael are not those holy, shining ones who have remained steadfast since their creation but are rather those human ones who have fallen and have since had to be reclaimed through "the blood of the Lamb," those angels who do not yet behold the face of their Father in heaven but who know him only by faith and through "the word of their testimony," who are still stalked day and night by their satanic deceiver, "who accuses them day and night before our God." These are angels who do not yet enjoy uninterrupted peace and triumph but who must yet wage "war in heaven"—in that heaven which

4. See Luther's Predigt am Michaelistage of 1544, D. *Martin Luthers Werke* (Weimar: Herman Böhlaus Nachfolger, 1913), vol. 49, p. 578.
5. Or is it Pseudo-Augustine? See Homilia IX in *Sancti Aurelii Augustine, Opera Omnia,* in *Patrologiae Patrum Latinorum,* ed. by J. P. Migne (Paris, 1841), col. 2434.

their Lord has called the "kingdom of heaven," which is not "lo here or lo there" but is among them.

Of course, the exegetes who identified the "angels" in Revelation 12 with the church in history had no wish to displace those *other* angels. The same Luther, when preaching not on the epistle but on the gospel lection for Michaelmas, makes no effort either to allegorize or to demythologize Matthew 18:10: "In heaven their angels always behold the face of their Father who is in heaven." [6] Similarly, the same Maritain who inveighed against angelism could write his friend Cocteau, concerning "the angels that guard us," that "my own philosophy was deeply concerned with them" and "it never tired of admiring the angelic natures." [7] On the other hand, his wife Raïssa wrote a charming book about a very down-to-earth angel, Thomas Aquinas, *The Angel of the Schools*.[8] Likewise the seer of the Apocalypse, who certainly had nothing against celestial angels, (1:1,2) nevertheless recorded his vision for an altogether human "angel of the church in Ephesus" (2:1) and "the angel of the church in Smyrna." (2:8) He could quite as easily have addressed it to the angels of the church in Pittsburgh or Saint Louis. Let us say then, at least for the purposes of our discussion, that the angels of Michael are you and I and all the church, and our "war in heaven" is the spiritual combat of the church militant.

Then who is this leader of the angels who is called Michael? According to the same exegetical tradition, the name "Michael" in this case does not refer to the angel Michael in the Book of Daniel, unless it be that angel of

6. *Op. cit.*, vol. 37, pp. 151–153.

7. Jacques Maritain and Jean Cocteau, tr. by John Coleman, *Art and Faith* (New York: Philosophical Library, 1948), p. 74.

8. "Saint Thomas, to tell the truth, was not invisible. He was even very tall, and very big. But like an angel he was pure and strong and a messenger of divine light." Raïssa Maritain, tr. by Julie Kernan, *St. Thomas Aquinas, The Angel of the Schools* (New York: Sheed and Ward, 1935), p. 12.

whom Nebuchadnezzar exclaimed, his form is like that "of the Son of God" (Daniel 3:25). The word Michael, in other words, might well not be a personal, creaturely name at all, like Gabriel or Peter or Paul, but in this case should rather be taken literally as a christological pun: *Micha-el*, "Who is like God," *Quis sicut Deus*. And who *is* like God? Earlier in the Book of Revelation John had spoken of "one like a son of man," (1:13) who is "the first and the last and the living one" (1:17,18) and "who loves us and has freed us from our sins by his blood and made us a kingdom, priests to his God and Father" (1:5,6). Which one is it of all the angels who himself so partakes of the divine majesty that he alone can be said to be truly the Son of God? Of whom does the writer to the Hebrews say, "he reflects the glory of God and bears the very stamp of his nature, upholding the universe by his word of power" (1:13)? This is he, the same epistle says, "who by himself purged our sins." Of whom does the writer to the Colossians say, "he is the image of the invisible God, the firstborn of all creation"? It is he "in whom we have redemption, the forgiveness of sins" (1:15,14).

From the outset, at least as early as Justin Martyr, "angel" was used as a christological title, and the Canon of Hippolytus celebrated "Christ the angel of great counsel." [9] Later exegetes explicitly identified Christ with the Michael of Revelation 12.[10] In the Augustinian sermon

9. Phillip Carrington, *The Meaning of the Revelation* (New York: Macmillan, 1931), p. 223. Augustine writes, "No one should be astonished to hear Christ spoken of as 'the angel of the Lord of hosts.'" *The City of God*, tr. by G. G. Walsh and D. J. Honan (New York: Fathers of the Church, Inc., 1954), Bk. XVIII, ch. 35, p. 140.

10. It can hardly be claimed, however, that this tradition achieved anything like unanimity. Speaking of Primasius, Pierre Prigent says, "La solide culture biblique de Primase lui interdit d'identifier Michaël au Christ." *Apocalypse 12, Histoire de l'exegese*, vol. 2 in *Beiträge zur Geschichte der biblischen Exegese* (Tübingen: J. C. B. Mohr, 1959), p. 20.

referred to earlier, the preacher tells his hearers, " . . . Michaelem, Christum intellige." [11] And for Beatus, says Prigent, "Michael n'est autre que le Christ." [12] Likewise for the Venerable Bede, who acknowledges his debt to Tyconius.[13] Nicholas of Lyra, to whom Luther owed much, may have intended the same identification when he referred to Michael as "Hercules" and as the vicar of God.[14] So perhaps did John Purvey, the Wycliffite, for whose commentary on the Apocalypse Luther wrote a Vorrede in 1528.[15] Sixteen years later Luther was still preaching:

> Der Fürst aber dieses Kriegs, den er Michael heisset, der ist und kann kein ander sein weder unser Herr Jhesus Christus, Gottes Sohn.[16]

Long after Luther Christians continued to sing Nikolaus Hermann's "Heut' singt die liebe Christenheit," which in one of its variants retains the identification, "Michael, unser Herre Christ." [17] Recently Wilhelm Koepp reported a revival of interest in the Michael-Christ tradition.[18]

Even exegetes who may not make the identification of Michael with Christ explicit do explicitly identify Michael's victory with Christ's. New Testament scholar Heinrich Schlier, formerly Lutheran and now Roman Catholic, has contributed a monograph to the fine series, "Quaestiones Disputatae," which numbers Leonard Swid-

---

11. Loc. cit.
12. Prigent, op. cit., p. 16.
13. The Complete Works of Venerable Bede, ed. by J. A. Giles (London: Whittaker, 1884), vol. XII, pp. 391–392.
14. Prigent, op. cit., p. 47.
15. Luther, op. cit., vol. 26, pp. 121–123.
16. Ibid. vol. 49, p. 578.
17. Wilhelm Stählin, Predigthilfen über die altkirchlichen Episteln, (Kassel: Johannes Stauda Verlag, 1955), p. 142.
18. "Christus, die Engel und Sankt Michael," Evangelisch-Lutherische Kirchenzeitung, vol. VI, nos. 20 and 21 (October 31 and November 15, 1952), pp. 367–369, 382–384.

ler among its contributors.[19] Entitled *Principalities and Powers in the New Testament,* Schlier's essay emphasizes repeatedly that the victory over Satan in Revelation 12, though it is "the victory of the heavenly powers," is one with "the victory of Christ"; that "the accuser and his accusation are thrust down from his place" because "the place before God's throne is taken by Jesus Christ who died and rose again"; and that the resultant hymn of triumph in Revelation 12 is "the effect of Christ's cross and resurrection." [20] In a series of lectures also entitled *Principalities and Powers* another exegete, G. B. Caird, notes that "in the main biblical tradition the fall of Satan from heaven coincides with the ministry of Jesus, and in particular with the Crucifixion." [21] By "the main biblical tradition" Caird means Revelation 12:10, but also Jesus' statements in Luke 10:18 ("I saw Satan fall like lightning from heaven") and in John 12:31 ("Now is the judgment of this world, now shall the ruler of this world be cast out.") It is Jesus then—at least let us say so for the problem at hand—who is the *Micha-el,* the *Quis sicut Deus,* whose angels we are. Christ and his church, Michael and all angels—a spiritual host whose ecumenical credentials ought to suffice. And Christians are unanimously ecumenical in confessing that only that Michael who is Christ is adequate to the spiritual warfare they confront.

The Church and the World Against the Common Enemy

In fact, the war his angels wage is more than ecumenical. (And war, let us repeat, is of the essence of their spirituality, not world-fleeing neutrality or appease-

19. Leonard Swidler (editor), *Dialogue for Reunion: The Catholic Premises* (New York: Herder and Herder, 1962).

20. *Principalities and Powers in the New Testament* (New York: Herder and Herder, 1961), pp. 73, 64, 47, 49.

21. *Principalities and Powers* (Oxford: Clarendon Press, 1956), p. 31.

ment or aloofness, however religious.) The spiritual warfare of the angels of Michael, at least on its outermost front, finds them joining forces not only with one another in the church but with all humanity as well, trans-ecumenically, in common cause against that hideous strength: "the great dragon, . . . that old serpent called the Devil and Satan." For he is bent upon the devestation not only of the angels of Michael, "our brethren," but of "the earth," "the whole world." His incursions are not confined to matters religious or even moral. He is equally adept with the seemingly secular weapons of disease and death and ignorance and poverty and dirt and unemployment and blight and violence. Melanchthon, in his hymn for Michaelmas, says of the Devil

> So now he subtly lies in wait
> To ruin school and church and state.[22]

Notice, not only church but school and state as well. Schlier writes:

> He takes possession of all levels of natural everyday life, . . . in the soul and body of the individual or in what we call natural phenomena, . . . in the general spirit of the world, or in the spirit of a particular period, attitude, nation or locality.[23]

In this battle the National Science Foundation and the holy Christian church, the pastor in his pulpit and the college physics instructor, the believer at his prayers and the reporter on his beat, the confessor with his absolution and the mother with her caresses and cures and consolations, the Christian demonstrator with his plac-

22. *The Lutheran Hymnal* (Saint Louis: Concordia Publishing House, 1941), no. 254.
23. Schlier, *op. cit.*, p. 31.

ard and the agnostic demonstrator with his, the paro-
chial-school teacher with the Bill of Rights and the
public-school teacher with the Pledge of Allegiance, the
church choir and the dancer and the clown, all are
comrades in arms against a common foe. To wage war
against this diabolic force is the responsibility not only of
the church but of every social institution, of every man
of good will, of all the arts and sciences and of every
useful endeavor. But the church does have a responsibility here, too, however ambiguous and problematical
that responsibility may become in her alliances with the
world. The very locale of this seminar, a church-related
university, is a parable in point. Here the church is engaged, of all things, in such apparently secular pursuits
as the identifying of isotopes, the conjugation of French
verbs, dating the Ming dynasty, brain-picking Freud and
Darwin and Nietzsche. On this perimeter of the battle—
which for the angels of Michael is no less spiritual, since
here too it is in his name that they strive—their alliances
are trans-ecumenical.

Not for a moment does this mean, however, that the
uniquely spiritual resource which the church marshals
against the adversary is obliterated. Not at all. That is
evident already in her reconnaissance. She knows the
enemy and, knowing him, she does not underestimate
him. That is why she calls out to her unwitting comrades
beyond the church, "woe to you, O earth and sea," not as
self-congratulation but as the eschatological warning.
She knows, even when the New Testament speaks of
"spirit against the flesh," that the spiritual struggle is not
finally against "flesh and blood" but against "principalities
and powers, against the world rulers of this present darkness" (Eph. 6:12). "The deceiver of the whole world"
is at his worst when he blinds the world to his very
existence, and hence to the urgency of its own need.

> To act, think or speak against this spirit is regarded as
> non-sensical or even as wrong and criminal. It is "in"
> this spirit that men encounter the world and affairs,
> which means that they accept the world as this spirit
> presents it to them, with all its ideas and values, in the
> form in which he wants them to find it.[24]

In the realm of letters Maritain observes a similar de-
monization, and issues his warning. "The unconcealed
and palpable influence of the devil on an important part
of contemporary literature is one of the significant phe-
nomena of the history of our time." [25]

The biologist who labors to isolate and classify some
deadly virus is reconnoitering, not only the enemy the
virus, but also "that old serpent called the Devil," who
knows even better than the biologist how to use viruses.
Now of course no one here is advocating that the biologist relinquish the germ theory of disease and go chasing
off after demons—which, no doubt, is exactly the way
they would best elude him. What we are suggesting is
that it would be better for the biologist, not for his biology
perhaps but surely for his theology, if he recognized that
his battle not only involves antibiotic versus virus but
also involves the Lord of life against the dragon of death.

The agronomist who has forgotten the curse which
was hurled at his ancestor in Eden, the curse of the
thorns and the thistles, the geologist who is unmindful
that the mountains can be invoked to fall on us and the
hills to cover us, the psychiatrist who ignores the hidden truth about demonic possession, the psychologist
who describes the phenomenon of learning and error
without giving a thought to the "father of lies"—is in
each case probably no worse off as a scientist. He may
even be better off than his Christian colleague, because

24. *Ibid.*, pp. 31–32.   ,
25. *Art and Scholasticism, op. cit.*, p. 108.

he is less distracted. And he is still, indeed, a useful ally against the forces of darkness. Nonetheless, he is a soldier who does not begin to know what he is up against, a soldier who might well win the battle but is doomed to lose the war.

We have come a long way in our secular culture since the days when our Nordic and Teutonic ancestors were tempted to see a demon or a troll or a sprite behind every bush, but our emancipation has cost us something, too. We have lost sight of the enemy, and that itself is a kind of bedevilment. The Robin Hood on our television screens today is still agile enough at tree-climbing and archery to delight our youngsters, but he no longer means either for us or for our youngsters what he once meant for the superstitious pagans of Old England, the struggle of the religious hero against the dark forces of the forest. If the factory workers of Derbyshire and Leek until recently have imagined that physical power needs not only machinery but incantations and gestures to domesticate it, *we* at least have long been too sophisticated to believe that. My contemporaries and I can no longer appreciate the attitude of a Luther who, when he made his journey to Rome, found the Alps (as others of his contemporaries did) a forbidding sight. We are more likely to see in them only what Rousseau did, enrapturing splendor and quietude for the soul.

As one physicist has noted, we have labored diligently and gratefully over the principle of evolution and have seen in it all sorts of optimistic implications for cosmic progress and human advance. Not nearly so diligently have we asked about the sobering implications of the principle of entropy, the irreversible tendency of physical events from order to disorder.[26] The very festival of

26. C. F. von Weizsäcker, tr. by Marjorie Grene, *The World View of Physics* (Chicago: The University of Chicago Press,

Michaelmas for which this epistle lesson was appointed is traditionally celebrated in the fall of the year because that is the time when day and night are in equilibrium, as Michael and the Dragon are in deadlock, and when the autumnal storms which are beginning to rage on the high seas betoken the struggle between the angels of God and the angels of Satan. We today are more apt to schedule Michaelmas at this particular time, if we do at all, because that is when the church publisher has scheduled it on the liturgical calendar. We have effectively demythologized Robin Hood and our factory machinery and the Alps and the second law of thermodynamics and the Feast of St. Michael—and not without immense benefit, let us admit it. However, there is the danger that the devils thus exorcised may have returned through the back door, more sanitary perhaps but seven times stronger than at first.

The blame for this new secular variety of bedevilment, to which we are so vulnerable because we are so unaware, does not lie with the secularist alone. Frequently his most cooperative accomplice is the church. She, too, is implicated in this fallacy, and not only when she is inclined to be too secular. Sometimes in diametric reaction to "the world" she abandons the battle and cowers within the sanctuaries of a false spirituality, too repelled by the raucous and uncouth clamor even to call out her "woes." What better way to surrender the field to the enemy? Pierre Pourrat, despite his unfortunate mispresentation of the Reformation, might well be correct in this observation:

> It was indeed . . . the desire to keep the spiritual life
> free from the pagan spirit of the Renaissance that

1952), pp. 167–171. For an alternative view of the matter, see Stephen Toulmin, "Contemporary Scientific Mythology," in *Metaphysical Beliefs,* ed. by Alasdaire MacIntyre and R. G. Smith (London: SCM press, 1957).

resulted in the development of methodical prayer. As the Christian found himself surrounded with nothing but enticements to evil, he had to fall back upon himself and encircle himself with the rampart of a method of prayer. He thus made a sort of inner sanctuary, closed to all unwholesome influences, and in it his supernatural convictions were guarded and fortified.[27]

However, if Pourrat means to construe this development in Christian spirituality as a blessing, even a mixed blessing, there is much too much historical evidence of churchly retreat and much too little of spiritual aggressiveness to warrant his optimism.

Let it be remembered that this retreat of the churches was not confined to one or two sectors of Christendom. What Pourrat reports about Roman Catholic spirituality had its parallels elsewhere. The noted Calvinist preacher at Charenton, Charles Drelincourt, reminded his seventeenth century hearers what it should mean for them to be "strangers" in the world. "The Strangers are not very fond of the land in which they are ill-used, and they speak of it only with scorn." [28] "Thus it comes about," remarks Albert-Marie Schmidt, "that Calvin's disciples actually break the explicit instructions of their master, and find pleasure in the doubtful luxury of a kind of religious segregation which has at times been wrongly encouraged by their ministers." [29]

As for the Lutherans, Werner Elert reports, "even those who could have had better knowledge made use of Luther's designation of the world as a 'vale of tears' in order to ascribe to Lutheranism an altogether quietistic-pessimistic conception of life."

27. *Christian Spirituality*, tr. by W. H. Mitchell (Westminster, Maryland: The Newman Press, 1953), vol. III, p. vi.

28. Quoted in Albert-Marie Schmidt, tr. by Robert Wallace, *Calvin and the Calvinist Tradition* (New York: Harper, 1960), p. 167.

29. *Ibid.*, p. 166.

Amid the joyful dawning of the Reformation one senses it in the sermons of Bugenhagen and later in the Latin sermons of Melanchthon or in the sermons Andreä preached against the Turks. Lukas Osiander opposed the calendar reform because, as he thought, the Last Day was near. . . . Tycho Brahe found that the new star that appeared on November 11, 1572, "had been shown to the world that was approaching its evening." And when the announcement was made at the Reformation jubilee in 1717 that the Saxon electoral prince had gone over to the Roman Church, the pastor at Leubnitz wrote to Löscher: "Evening is approaching; now, Christ, it shall remain ours."

"Of course," Elert adds, "the thought that the end of the world is imminent is common to . . . the Gospel. But the mood of doom of the sixteenth and seventeenth centuries is . . . brought about by inner-worldly details: the menacing comet, the danger from the Turks, or, as Melanchthon puts it, the 'catastrophes' of the Roman Empire." [30] For that matter who of us cannot sympathize with these fathers in the faith? Nor is it for us to poke the accusing finger at them. But there is such a thing as being warned by their experience and remembering, in fear and trembling, that if these things be done in a green tree what could be done in a dry one?

The alternative is to welsh on the world. Far too often a false spirituality, retrenched and gun-shy, has abandoned the church's secularist allies, who then have to go it alone, unmindful of the real odds and the real adversary. It was not only to the Dominicans but to all the angels of Michael that Camus made his conscience-searing plea. "Perhaps we cannot prevent this world from being a world in which children are tortured. But

30. *The Structure of Lutheranism,* tr. by Walter A. Hansen (Saint Louis: Concordia Publishing House, 1962), vol. I, pp. 464–465.

we can reduce the number of tortured children. And if you don't help us, who else in the world can . . .?"

> . . . A great unequal battle has begun. . . . But I believe it must be fought, and I know that certain men at least have resolved to do so. I merely feel that they will occasionally feel somewhat alone, that they are in fact alone. . . . And what I know . . . is that if Christians made up their minds to it, millions of voices—millions, I say—throughout the world would be added to the appeal of a handful of isolated individuals. . . .[31]

While saints are at their prayers burly sinners have to run the world.

In this perimeter of the battle where church and non-church are united against the same enemy, the very least to be expected is that there will be cooperation between Christian and Christian, church and church, regardless of their confessional differences. "This concern with the problem of the modern world," writes Robert McAfee Brown, "provides the area in which Roman Catholics and non-Roman Catholics can most immediately begin to make common cause together."

> Catholics and Protestants can sit around a mayor's table together and urge revision of discriminatory housing statutes, even though they cannot yet sit around the Lord's Table, eating one bread and drinking from one cup. Catholics and Protestants can agree about the dogma that every man, regardless of the color of his skin, is made in God's image, even though they cannot yet agree about the dogma of the Assumption of the Virgin Mary.[32]

31. Albert Camus, tr. by Justin O'Brien, *Resistance, Rebellion, and Death* (New York: The Modern Library, 1960), pp. 55–56.
32. "Protestant Hopes for the Vatican Council," *Look,* vol. 28, no. 20 (October 6, 1964), p. 23.

The truth is that this minimal "common cause" is trans-ecumenical, engaging not only "Catholics and Protestants" but all men, extending as it does far beyond the battle lines of the Christian church. There are numberless opportune ways in which the angels of Michael share the cause also with the non-Christian and the worldling and "the unspiritual man," and it is no tribute to our spirituality, and no advantage to the battle of Michael, if we depreciate the divine boon of the secularist ally and the chance to aid and succor him—not least with the warning to him, "woe to you, O earth and sea, for the devil has come down to you in great wrath, because he knows that his time is short." It is right and proper, therefore, that John XXIII's *Pacem in Terris* should invite cooperation with "all men of good will," "also with human beings who are not enlightened by faith in Jesus Christ, but who are endowed with the light of reason and with a natural and operative honesty." [33]

The Spirituality of Accusation

However, there is still that one most lethal form of satanic harassment which the church, and the church uniquely, is called to cope with. The seer of the Apocalypse refers to this when he calls the Devil "the accuser" who day and night accuses the brethren before God. It is by his accusations more than by anything else that Satan succeeds, as the seer says, in deceiving the whole world. Of what does he accuse the brethren? He accuses them of sin—for instance, the sin of inter-denominational lovelessness. But what is so satanic about that accusation? They really are sinful, really loveless and

33. The complete text of the encyclical, in official English translation, appeared in *Saint Louis Review,* special supplement, April 19, 1963. See p. 7.

distant, aren't they? Indeed they are, grievously so. The trouble is, the adversary does his accusing not by innuendo or by private revelations but by the facts, by the public and palpable circumstances of history. For example, the churches' lovelessness stands accused by something so real as their existing institutional divisions. Yes, but doesn't that incriminating evidence simply confirm the Devil's accusations more than ever? True, yet his accusations, especially since they have the ring of hard fact, deceive men into believing it is God who is accusing them, as though their lovelessness angers God, as though their strife and their rifts are a divine judgment upon them. Ah, but their rifts are a divine judgment, and a wrathful one, too. There is plenty of biblical warrant for that.

If that is so, then ponder the consequences for our spirituality. If the Devil's accusations embody the judgment of the holy God, then the manly thing to do, it would seem, is not to complain about how satanic and deceitful these accusations are but rather to take them seriously as godly and truthful and to make maximum spiritual use of them, however much the painful truth may hurt. Doesn't it follow, in other words, that this accusatory self-criticism not only is needed but is in truth the answer, the divine answer, to our need? Isn't this exactly the kind of spirituality which good ecumenists should urge: to face up to the grim facts of our brokenness, and not only to face up to these facts but to drive them home, each one of us out-confessing the other; to make no premature boasts about our unity, except perhaps that of the "invisible church," and never to glory in our inter-confessional gains lest we grow complacent and self-deceived; to let the deserved accusations do their penitential work, reducing our self-sufficiency to an honest acceptance of our finitude and need; until finally, the last veil of self-deception fallen, we are united—as sinners, if nothing else?

Is that finally the answer? No, not finally, at least not God's. Satan's final answer, yes, but not Michael's. Yet Satan's answer, just because his accusations are vastly and factually true and humanly impossible to refute and in line with the very judgment of God, seduces the most spiritual and the most ecumenical of men, the "saintly" ones as well as the "practical" ones, the "angelists" as well as the "anglers" to recall that outrageous pun of Gregory I (who was "the Great" obviously in spite of his pun) about the angelic Angles. Both types of spirituality are prone to satanism—literally, to accusationism. The ecclesiastical pragmatists, on the one hand, who work all the angles, those problem-solvers and trouble-shooters who sometimes qualify euphemistically as "churchmen" —as distinguished, presumably, from plain church members—exercise a spirituality which for all its activism is basically negative. It proceeds at the outset from what is *wrong* with the church. That is, it proceeds from an accusation. To proceed instead from what is right with the church and from that glorious success and unity she already enjoys is, from the nervous viewpoint of the anglers, the fatal road to complacency and stagnation. Their spirituality affirms the way of accusation with a frenetic and elaborately programmed, but sadly mistaken, Yes.

Still, if the answer to the Accuser is not Yes, neither is it No. To say, Man does *not* live by accusation, is true but it is not the answer. For that, too, is but one more accusation, an accusation of our accusatoriness. That is like trying to be positive by saying, "We ought not be so negative." But that double negative does characterize the spirituality of the saintly "angelists," who are sick of

the endless criticisms and reforms and diagnoses, who
are impatient with the impatience of the ecumenists and
who respond with generous wrath to any mention of the
wrath of God and who find nothing so sinful as the
doctrine of original sin. They flee instead for their spirituality to a negation of the negatives, resembling in this
superficial respect the *via negativa* of those old mystics
who sought the One through reducing all consciousness
of the worldly Many to a psychic "Null." The assumption
evidently is that two No's make a Yes also in matters
spiritual—that is, that two deaths make a life. When
pressed to divulge just where the Yes is to be found—
where that church is, for example, which by their own
confession is one, holy, catholic and apostolic—the angelists point off and away to some "invisible church,"
"dreaming about some Platonic republic" as Melanchthon says,[34] or they point to a oneness among Christians
which so far prevails only in the divine love or only "in
Christ," the implication being that none of this transcendent unity is yet to be seen and heard in the facts of
churchly existence, down here where the negating is
being done and where it needs to be undone.

However, if the answer to the Accuser is neither Yes
nor No, and surely it is not some little bit of both, then
that appears to exhaust every alternative. Yet that very
appearance is the great satanic deception, namely, that
there is no other way than the way of self-criticism or
the way of the criticism of self-criticism, at least no other
way which is godly and spiritual and ecumenical. But
that assumption is, to call it by its biblical name, a lie.
Nevertheless, to say even that, true as it may be, is only
another denunciation. Where is there an authentic, all-

34. "Apology of the Augsburg Confession," in T. G. Tappert
(tr. and ed.), *The Book of Concord* (Philadelphia: Muhlenberg
Press, 1959), p. 171.

displacing Yes? Where on earth—yes, on earth—is that church which is one, holy, catholic and apostolic? Where is there an already flourishing spirituality which defeats the Accuser, not by trying to outdo his accusations nor by surrendering the earth to him, not even by declaring war against him, but by declaring victory over him? Wherever that is, then there, we can be sure, is the real spirituality for ecumenism.

Before we proceed to that resolution, however, the reminder is in order that the accusations of Satan, including his exposures of our unchurchliness, reflect at the same time the effectual judgment of God. There is nothing so pathetically naive as the church which forgets on whose authority the accusations ultimately come and which supposes that the accusations can be dispelled if the brethren would only stop believing them and would please be a little more positive. 'As though the accusations originated in the heads of the brethren. 'As though the hard fact that you are Presbyterians and you are Roman Catholics and I am a Lutheran, that your children had best not inter-marry with mine, that your Roman bishops are deprived of the admonitions of your Reformed presbyteries, that we mean contrary things when we confess the same words, that you may not commune at my altar, that your fonts are not for our infants or my alms for your needy or your prayers for our missionaries—as though these hard facts of life and death needed nothing more to eradicate them than you and I, or even you and I and all other Christians, should decide to do so. 'As though these facts had nothing at all to do with the very judgment of God. 'As though nothing more were needed to reverse his judgment than that we should decide to do so.

Already in the ancient story of Balaam, Caird reminds us, "the function of the *satan* is to oppose the wrongdoer, and it is a divine function." [35] Also "throughout the New Testament period Satan retains his juridical duties. . . . As long as there are sinners to be arraigned before the judgment seat of God, there is work for Satan in heaven." [36] "In heaven," of course, does not imply that his accusations are removed from the factuality of our common existence, where we do in fact make decisions and where our decisions do make some difference in fact. "The 'heavens' . . . surround and touch upon the material world . . .," says Schlier. "By the heavens we mean the supreme form of material life; it is the Unseen which we nevertheless perceive, . . . by which [man] is menaced, seduced and determined." [37] Nevertheless, though the accusations of Satan are played out within the immanent circumstances of our history, where we act as well as are acted upon, it is first of all "before our *God*," says the seer, that the accusations are conducted. Hence, if ecumenism is not to be ruined by a spirituality of negation, if the way of accusation is to be overcome, then it must be overcome "in heaven," "before our God," as well as in the decisions and acts of our churchly life.

Alas, even to say "the way of accusation *must* be overcome" only re-enforces a prior accusation, namely, that as yet it has *not* been overcome. Our most pious imperatives only barely conceal the satanic (though divine) negatives which they presuppose, and in effect these imperatives reinstate the round of accusation more firmly than before. What a snare is the adversary's web! Every exertion against it only constricts it the more. The tightening circle may begin, for instance, with a well-meaning lament over our churches' dividedness. But then, pricked by the reminder of what fellowship we do

35. Caird, *op. cit.*, p. 31.
36. *Ibid.*, p. 33.
37. Schlier, *op. cit.*, p. 17.

enjoy, we apologize for our ingratitude. That is, we criticize our criticalness. But to that second round of criticism, just by my exposing it, I have now added a third criticism. And there in turn, by exposing myself, I have compounded the third with a fourth, and now that one with still another, *ad infinitum*. This is not the sophistry, the game of words, which at first it seems to be. Unfortunately not. (But even if it were, that would only be meeting the problem with still another criticism.) Nor can the deadly circle be eluded simply by translating our spirituality from negative sentences into affirmatives, as though it were all but a matter of syntax. Even such a positive, smiling announcement as "We in the ecumenical movement have so much to be thankful for" still implies the accusation, "Yes, and that only reveals how very thankful we ought to be but are not." To dispose of the accusation altogether we would have to be able to announce, "We in the ecumenical movement are every bit as thankful as we ought to be." But that rash claim, in face of all withering accusations to the contrary, we dare not make. Understandably not.

The vicious circle, far from being merely a secular accident of language or a psychological case of excessive scrupulosity, is as cosmic as that demonic ring of evil which the witches of old supposed could be broken only by exceptionally superior and secret powers. Biblically, as in the second chapter of Romans, this vortex of accusation upon accusation, criticism upon criticism—Paul uses the same word, *krima*—is the inescapably immanent way in which the righteous God causes sinners to implicate themselves in the divine judgment precisely by their invoking it. And the more conscientious and dis-*crimi*-nating and judgmental they are, the more in-*crimi*-nated they are. "O man, whoever you are, when you judge another, . . . in passing judgment upon him you condemn yourself." (2:1) That being so, the solution would then seem to be (also in the churches' ecumenical practice) to stop passing judgment upon "another" and to start judging themselves. Still, that is only a subtler form of the same judgment, perhaps just a more advanced stage of the critical spiral. Like those "who have not the law," their very *self*-criticisms

> show that what the law requires is written on their hearts, while their conscience also bears witness and their conflicting thoughts accuse or perhaps excuse them. . . .

Their accusing themselves—indeed, even their excusing themselves—only confirms the unbroken *krima* of God himself, as "God judges the secrets of men . . ." (2:14–16). Thus, whether they criticize others or criticize themselves or criticize their criticism of others or their criticism of themselves, they themselves perpetuate (as I am doing this very moment) the whole deadly order of the law, the satanic spirituality of accusation.

The Circle Is Broken by the Blood of the Lamb

How is the fatal circle broken? "By the blood of the Lamb," the seer of the Apocalypse exults, thereby divulging the vital secret, the *mysterion*. Our ecumenism is as spiritual—that is, as triumphant over the adversary —and our spirituality is as ecumenical—that is, as cosmic in its victory—as both our ecumenism and our spirituality enjoy "the blood of the Lamb." Enjoy, indeed. The cross and the blood and the hill called The Skull and the Agnus Dei, though they sound for all the world like No, (and may sound that way also to the angelists and the anglers) are the one jubilant Yes of the angels of Michael everywhere. For the satanic law of accusation, in fact God's own law, which "increases trespass" and

"brings wrath" and "kills," God himself has undergone,
"made of a woman, made under the law," "made a curse
for us," "made to be sin for us," bearing "our sin in his
body on the tree," "condemning sin in the flesh." Sub-
mitting to the deadly circle of the divine *krima*, he suffered it out of existence, burst it asunder, new wine for
old wineskins, the yeast of joy for the bread of sorrows,
grace for law, forgiveness for accusation, new covenant
for old—all of it "in my blood."

This theme of "the blood of the Lamb", perhaps more
pervasively and ecumenically than any other, informs
the spirituality of Christian churches everywhere: in
Bach's *Saint Matthew Passion* and the Salvation Army's
"Are you Washed in the Blood of the Lamb," in a pastor's
signing his flock with the cross or in a young girl's neck-
lace with the cross as her yoke, in a massive, abstract
crucifix or in a humble peasant's icon, in "dying with
Christ" in baptism whether in a Tennessee River or in a
cathedral baptistry, in the burial liturgies for those who
are "laid to rest in the Lord," in the Nicene Creed's "he
suffered and was buried" and in every collect's "for Jesus'
sake," and especially in the Holy Communion of his body
and blood.

As the church's spirituality equally attests, "the blood
of the Lamb," for all its abject humiliation, is not for
that reason any less a victory. Good Friday is of a piece
with Easter, not a prologue to it, not some traumatic
episode which on Easter Sunday the church hastens to
forget as though our Lord's death were the opposite of his
resurrection. Rather, in the wondrous dialectic of the
Easter Preface, the church speaks of him "who by his
death hath destroyed death and by his rising again hath
restored to us everlasting life"—giving praise "for the
glorious resurrection" of whom? "The very Paschal Lamb

which was offered for us." In the gospel for the first Sunday after Easter the risen Lord who appears to doubting Thomas still bears the nail-prints and the scar (John 20:25–38), a sign if ever there was that the victory had gone his way: the way of the good shepherd who lays down his life for the sheep (John 10:11). At mass on the third Sunday after Easter the Alleluia Verse celebrates the same mysterious connection: "It behooved Christ to suffer these things and so to enter his glory, alleluia." Even on Pentecost, when the congregation sings full-throat Rhabanus Maurus' ninth century "Veni Creator Spiritus," unable to contain the exultation of the doxological stanza without springing to their feet, young and old alike, they still sing, "The Savior Son be glorified, who for lost men's redemption died." At the throne where Isaiah had only seen "the Lord . . . high and lifted up," (6:1) the seer of the Apocalypse saw with better vision "a Lamb," who receives the "new song": ". . . thou wast slain and by thy blood didst ransom men for God" (5:6,9). This song of the blood of the Lamb the church still echoes, and always on a note of triumph, in her *Dignus est Agnus.*

Through the Cross Comes the Forgiveness of Sins

"The blood of the Lamb"—for all its apparent irrelevance to those ecumenical programmers who are wont to say of it, "Yes, but now to get practical . . ."—is the very thing which marks the spirituality of the angels of Michael as "power" and "authority." What the "loud voice in heaven" announced to the seer was that "the power . . . of our God and the authority of his Christ have come." It is this advent of "the authority of his Christ," an advent already accomplished, for which the "practical" anglers still pathetically wait, as for Godot,

and for which they still negotiate. Like the scribes in the
ninth chapter of Matthew they need to hear that "the
Son of Man has authority upon earth. . . ."

Perhaps their discontent is with the *function* of his
authority, "to forgive sins," (Mt. 9:6) as though that
were still something less than victory over the adversary.
Yet that is the very point at which the Accuser has been
vanquished, namely, at that point where the paralytic is
told, "Take heart, my son, your sins are forgiven" (9:2).
To say also, "Rise, take up your bed and go home," is not
some second, different species of authority. It is but an
extension of the one "authority upon earth to forgive
sins" (9:6). To conquer viruses and segregation and
poverty and ignorance, as we insisted earlier, is surely
the winning of crucial battles. But to do so without de-
feating the ultimate adversary, the Accuser, by means
of the ultimate weapon, "the blood of the Lamb"—to
heal the paralytic without forgiving his sin—is to win
the battle and yet lose the war. Similarly, the authority
which alone heals the paralysis and wounds in the
church is not our negotiated mergers, not even the ones
which result from ardent prayer and doctrinal agree-
ments and unanimous votes, (indispensable as these
are) but rather that authority which frees the churches
from every accusation, including the accusation of their
dividedness: "the authority of the Son of Man upon
earth to forgive sins."

Yet isn't it just that, namely that clearing the churches
of accusation, which ecumenical anglers dread as ruin-
ous permissivness lulling churches into ecumenical
drones? That is a risk, let us admit it, especially where
the prior accusations of the adversary are mistaken for
merely human self-criticism, for something less fearful
than the judgment of God. But there is a greater risk.
By pretending that Christ does not already and in fact

unite the churches in exonerating them of their divisions, we leave the churches with nothing but that penultimate authority: divine "criticism"—which word also means, originally, to separate. The really ecumenical sprituality is the one which, on good "authority," sings out in the midst of its empirical divisions, "Who shall lay any charge against God's elect, . . . who shall separate us from the love of Christ" (Rom. 8:33,35)? Recall the words of the absolution, not in their still somewhat tentative and guarded form as at prime or lauds or compline, "May the almighty and merciful Lord grant us pardon," etc., but in a bold and declaratory formula like this one:

> Upon this your confession I, by virtue of my office as a called and ordained servant of the Word, announce the grace of God unto all of you, and in the stead and by the command of my Lord Jesus Christ I forgive you all your sins in the name of the Father and of the Son and of the Holy Ghost.[38]

It is not impractical wishfulness, surely, but "the authority of his Christ" which in that superbly ecumenical act of spirituality, the *Apostolicum*, conjoins "the holy catholic church, the communion of saints" immediately with "the forgiveness of sin."

On the other hand, perhaps what they object to who underestimate the forgiveness of sin is not only that it is impractical and powerless but also that it is an easy way out. Easy, indeed. "Which is easier," Jesus asks the scribes, to forgive the paralytic or to heal him (Mt. 9:5)? We dare not miss the devastating irony in his question. "Easy," indeed. If only the scribes and all those law-oriented anglers who assume divine forgiveness is self-evident and, finding *such* forgiveness too easy, need to implement it with "accusation" and cajolery—if they

38. *The Lutheran Hymnal, op. cit.,* p. 16.

only knew how "easy" it really was to get the paralytic's sin forgiven. It was as "easy" as the cross. It was, as Matthew had just explained, (Mt. 8:17) that "easy" way of Isaiah's suffering servant, the *ebed yahweh* who removes "our iniquities . . . and our diseases" by "bearing" them and "taking" them as his own, not simply by revealing a forgiveness which would have prevailed anyway whether Jesus had borne the sin or not.

"There is no forgiveness of sins," says the Epistle to the Hebrews, "without the shedding of blood" (9:22). Whether Hebrews qualifies as canonical or not, the "blood" which refutes the easiness of Christ's forgiveness looms large enough right within the gospel of Matthew. As the passion history moves to its climax, we are brought to the supper in the upper room where Jesus makes unmistakably clear to his disciples by what "easy" way he secures their forgiveness: ". . . for this is my blood of the covenant, which is poured out for many for the forgiveness of sins" (26:28). Unfortunately there are those poor, bloodless traditions within the churches' spirituality whose eucharistic practice (if any) shrinks from the realism of our Lord's body and blood in the sacrament. What is unecumenical about that is not that it is a minority view (it may not be) but rather that it implies a forgiveness of sin which is available, easily enough, without "the blood of the Lamb." 'As though divine forgiveness were some timeless truth which would obtain anyway, with or without Jesus Christ, and which needs him at all not to bring the forgiveness about but only to bring it to light. In that case his absolving the paralytic really would have been as easy (and as ineffectual?) as his words, "take heart." 'As though this forgiveness did not need massive authorization, the *exousia* of the cross, in order to displace a whole cosmic order to the contrary, an order of accusation and divine judgment.

What is unspiritual finally about such christologies and their attendant eucharists, which so barely need the cross at all, is their reactionary regression to the way of the adversary, to a spirituality of accusationism rather than hard-won victory. The Lord's Supper, of course, is more than absolution, (it is also communion and eucharist and sacrifice) and there is also absolution without the Lord's Supper. But in this sacrament of bread and wine together with our Lord's *verba* concerning his body and blood—perhaps the earliest quotation we have from him (I Cor. 11:23–25)—the spirituality of the Christian *oikumene* best dramatizes the oneness of forgiveness and the cross. That this forgiveness was not easy to come by is directly related to its authority, as "the authority of his Christ" is related to "the blood of the Lamb."

Now it may be that we have still not met the real point of the angler's objection. Perhaps what he objects to is that forgiveness of sin is an easy way out, not for Christ admittedly, who by the critic's own Christian confession did indeed bear the cross, but for *Christians,* who presumably bear none of that cross and who ought not be coddled with cheap grace. This argument has considerable warrant, both sad and glad. 'Glad, because the church joyfully admits that the burden she has inherited from her Lord is, as he promised, "light" and his yoke "easy" (Mt. 11:30). Her yoke is easy because it is his before it is hers, and the church's spirituality abounds in reminders to this effect, particularly in her ministrations to the afflicted and the dying, and always and only to the penitent. What is sad, on the other hand, is not only that the forgiveness of sin seems to offer an easy way out but also, just because it does, it is for the man of conscience not the easiest but the very hardest thing on earth to accept. Witness the angler himself, *unable* to accept such an "easy" way out as forgiveness. His protest refutes itself. Easy, indeed. When was it, according to the words of consecration in the sacrament, that Jesus instituted the Lord's Supper? "The night when he was betrayed" (I Cor. 11:23). Betrayed by whom? Not only by Judas. After Judas had left the supper, the loyal disciples who stayed on that evening to receive the Lord's "blood of the covenant . . . poured out for . . . the forgiveness of sins" found the staying less and less easy. When time came for the outpouring, "then all the disciples forsook him and fled" (Mt. 26:56). Forgiveness is always cruciform, and it is this recurrent apostasy from it, not the acceptance of it, which every disciple finds alarmingly easy.

It is not to alarm him, however, but precisely to make forgiveness *easy* for him who is alarmed that the church mobilizes the full might of her spirituality: accusing and warning him, yes, but always again and again restoring him by that very power, ironically, from which he had apostatized, the easy yoke of forgiveness. Under that easy yoke all his other yokes of conscience—the needs and demands of his fellows, his afflictions and spiritual struggles, even the divine accusations—become light as well. They become light not in the sense that he ceases to feel their pressure, (he is not that kind of angel) but in the sense that he exploits their pressure to new purpose, bringing them into captivity under Christ, to serve the cause of forgiveness. These heavy, conscientious yokes become for him "the dear holy cross," as Luther called them—"holy," I suppose, because under their weight Christ's forgiveness is increasingly easy to want and enjoy, "dear" because the very accusations remind him of their opposite, the forgiveness of the Christ of the cross.

To sustain the *militia Christi* in this astute and supple spirituality the church's most staple supply-line no doubt is preaching, thus taking a cue from the apostles. Still, it is not only by the preacher that the Christian is fortified. He is surrounded and supported by the whole congregation, particularly at worship. The sin which burdens him they join in confessing. His petititons are gathered up, "collected," and are prayed in the common collect. If his own confession of faith is weak, it comes out strong in the one credal voice of the congregation. His singing improves as it is lost in theirs. It has been said of Lutheranism (and perhaps of other communions) that during the long famine of Rationalism, when the preaching was almost as arid as the theology, the people sustained one another with the hymnal and the liturgy. In every age of the church this purpose remains: What previously had been not only difficult but humanly impossible, namely to thrive on forgiveness and to venture boldly in its liberation, is exactly what the church wills to make easy for all who are "weary and heavyladen," rallying to them with the whole range of her spirituality.

The Unity of the Church

It has not escaped your notice, I am sure, that repeatedly we have been employing such locutions as "the church does this" or "the church does that." That is more than a manner of speaking. The bold thing about such an expression is not only that it assumes the church is singular—perhaps most Christians assume that, including the angelists with their "invisible" church—but also that it assumes the one church is actually *doing* this or that, already and upon earth. It is this assumption—better, this faith—which the angelist finds difficult to manage. (As we turn our attention now from the angler to the angelist, still apologizing for the poor pun, perhaps these two designations ought to be cleared of any misunderstandings they may have accumulated here: these "dear enemies," as Maritain might call them, are only ideal types, not photographic reproductions of actual Christians; moreover, they are not so much op- posites as they are converse sides of the same piety of accusationism; finally, they are probably not "they" at all but "we," the common temptation of every Christian.) What the angelist prefers to discount is that there is in fact a flourishing ecumenical spirituality, here and now, the agent of which is not so much the churches as the church, and not only Christ the head of the church but with him his body.

The locale for the authority of the Son of Man to forgive sin is, as he said, "upon earth" (Mt. 9:6). But what is more, the same authority upon earth which is his he shares upon earth with his disciples. It is no accident that, when Matthew concludes this healing story with a report on the crowd's reaction, he writes that "they glorified God, who had given such authority [not only to this man but] to *men*" (Mt. 9:8). Later on Jesus explains to these "men" how literally his authority is now theirs: "Truly, I say to you, whatever you bind on earth shall be bound in heaven, and whatever you loose on earth shall be loosed in heaven" (Mt. 18:18). Similarly, in our Michaelmas text, the accuser not only is displaced from the "place" where Michael and his angels happen to be but is displaced by the very act of Michael *and his angels.*" Of this text (12:10) Schlier explains:

> This implies that . . . the principalities can always be driven from the place which Jesus Christ occupies on this earth as well, from the "body of Christ," which is the Church.

To this we should add: the principalities are driven out not only *from* the church but, because she is that body whose head is Christ, also *by* the church. Of "our brethren" the seer writes: *"They* have conquered him by the blood of the Lamb and by the word of *their* testimony. . . ."

Their conquest, of course, is always "by the blood of the Lamb," but by invoking that Lamb in "the word of their testimony," it is "they," "our brethren," the church, to whom Christ's conquest is likewise ascribed. Really, to say the one is to say the other. If the forgiveness of sin accrues at the outset from something so firmly "upon earth" as the Son of Man's bearing sinners' sin and bleeding human blood, it is but an extension of that same wonder when he authorizes these sinners to perform his forgiveness with him. The reason it is hard to believe "the holy, catholic church, the communion of saints" (especially when the translation reads "the communicating of holy things") is fundamentally the same reason it is hard to believe "who for us men and for our salvation . . . suffered and was buried." And the church's spirituality deals with the one problem as with the other, by renewing the very assurances of gospel which are so incredible. When canon 82 of the Trullan Council (692) forbade the representation of Christ under the form of a lamb, (contrary to liturgical tradition and of course to biblical precedent) Sergius I, a Syrian, provided—in practical protest, some say—for the special singing of the Agnus Dei. By the eleventh century the church was singing, as she still is today, her "O Christ, thou Lamb of God" in threesomes.[39] How low the divine mercy stoops, whether in the lowly Lamb himself or in the authority to forgive which he shares with his lowlier brothers, needs constant reminder in the church's spirituality. A formula for private absolution at the time of the Reformation has the pastor asking, "Do you believe that the forgiveness I declare is the forgiveness of God?" The penitent

39. Cross, *op. cit.*, p. 26.

answers, "Yes, I do," and the absolution which follows both confirms his faith and confers what he believes: "Be it done for you as you have believed; according to the command of our Lord Jesus Christ, I forgive you your sins in the name of the Father," etc.[40] In this boldly realistic sense the word and sacraments of the church are, as the fathers called them, the very "means of grace."

That may well be: Our singing the *Agnus Dei* is itself the means by which the Lamb does "have mercy upon us," and it is nothing less than God's absolution which the penitent hears from his fellow-Christian. But we have still not made good on our promise: to identify an actual spirituality which is the doing, not only of this Christian or that Christian or of this church or that church, or the doing of Christ alone, but of his church as a whole, acting as one and upon earth. What if Sergius did sing the *Agnus Dei,* or even Sergius and a thousand Syrian Christians besides? That does not yet include the Christians at the Trullan Council, or for that matter the Presbyterians from Pittsburgh, not to mention "the whole church in earth and heaven." What if some Reformation pastors did forgive sin in the triune name? That is not all the pastors of the Reformation, much less a concensus of all the laymen, not only not in Rome and Byzantium but not even in Geneva and Wittenberg. Their pastoral practice had neither your approval nor mine nor the apostles'. All of us might have approved, of course, but none of us were consulted. Then how could the absolution of some obscure *Pfarrer* in Saxony or the *Kyrie* in some eleventh century convent or the evangelical sermon of a Scottish missionary in India or the Christian committal at a graveside in Hiroshima or a cup of water "in Jesus' name" in only-God-knows-where

40. Tappert, *op. cit.,* p. 351.

—how could any one of these actions realistically and with even minimal sense be said to be the action of the one, holy, catholic, and apostolic church? One thing is sure: if that could be said, then the one church could hardly be "invisible"; these very actions would render her visible and audible and palpable. Of course, that these actions not only could be but are the work of the triune God, at the same time that they are the work of this or that Christian, should not surprise anyone who knows how immanently that God works in Incarnation and Atonement and means of grace. But at the moment we are claiming something more, namely that these are the actions as well of the church of Christ one and entire, of Michael and all his angels, as ecumenical as any spirituality could be.

It is just this claim, however, which the seer of the Apocalypse presupposes when he says of those victorious martyrs, who "loved not their lives even unto death," that they are "our brethren." The fact that *they* have conquered [the accuser] by the blood of the Lamb and by the word of *their* testimony" gives cause to "rejoice," not only to them but to all "heaven and you that dwell therein." When they conquered, so did the whole church. In "the word of their testimony" they witnessed for the entire brotherhood. But then the brotherhood in that case must obviously not be the aggregate of all individual Christians in the world's history, since most Christians by far participated not at all in the "testimony" of those martyrs whom the seer describes. In fact, most Christians had not the remotest notion, nor have we to this day, who those martyrs were or what precisely they said, though they said it as our spokesmen! Still, the brotherhood is on record as having been there, as they spoke and as they died, and it shares the credit with unabashed rejoicing. The brotherhood, consequently, must be a single totality, not a sum total but a one total—or, to call it by a name which I confess is not original with me, a "body." And this body is not merely reducible to its constituent members, even though these members are the bearers in fact of the body's action. In fact, there is always the possibility that the action of the body may be carried out even by those who themselves are not genuine members but "hypocrites" and "hirelings." Even so, if it is truly the word and the sacraments which they declare and administer, then, as the church had to affirm against the Donatists, the action in question is still the validly Christian—ecumenical and spiritual—action of the body as a whole, independently of the motives of the individual bearers.

> Some indeed preach Christ from envy and rivalry, . . . not sincerely but thinking to afflict me in my imprisonment. What then? Only in that every way, whether in pretense or in truth, Christ is proclaimed; and in that I rejoice. (Phil. 1:15–18)

And so, with equal right, does the entire brotherhood, knowing as it does that wherever "the word of their testimony" invokes "the blood of the Lamb" there is a victory for the whole brotherhood. "Rejoice then, O heaven and you that dwell therein!"

On what grounds does the church speak of herself as a corporate unity, a living organism which is not limited to any one time or place and which bodies forth as a single agent in every action done in the name of Christ? Her grounds for this assurance are biblical and her biblical grounds, as usual, are christological. Christ "is the head of the body, the church" (I Col. 1:18). "Now you are the body of Christ and individually members of it" (I Cor. 12:27). The grounds of this assurance, to put it negatively, are not the general sociological observations of our age which have rediscovered the solidarity of social existence. Nor are they the biological models in Whitehead's or Alexander's philosophy of organism, or the newer field theory in the sciences, or the creaturely interdependence in the stories of Hemingway. On the other hand, it would be sheer ingratitude on the part of the church—an ingratitude which the Russian Christians, in their broad concept of *sobornost,* do not commit —not to acknowledge that, without these secular promptings, she might well have forgotten again the *soma tou Christou* in her own New Testament. Wise ecumenical theologians are making the most of the rediscovery, particularly of its christological justification.[41] ". . . Christ [cherishes] the church, because we are members of his body" (Eph. 5:30). ". . . We, though many, are one body in Christ, and individually members one of another" (Rom. 12:5).

How exclusively it is Christ whom the church needs in order to act as one body becomes evident, not from abstruse ontological descriptions of the church, but from her own most ordinary churchly action, her use of the means of grace, word and sacraments. The church is where Christ is, but Christ is where his means of grace are. "Where two or three are gathered in my name," he promises, "there am I in the midst of them" (Mt. 18:20). I take this to mean that two or three Christians who are riding in a crowded bus, no one of them aware of the others' Christianity or even of the others' presence, would not yet constitute the church in whose midst Christ promises to be. The church is constituted not by the mere existence of Christians in the world, however closely they may jostle one another, but rather by their being gathered in the explicit name of their Lord,

41. Robert S. Pelton, (editor) *The Church as the Body of Christ* (Notre Dame: University of Notre Dame Press, 1963).

around his word preached and his sacraments administered. The Augsburg Confession says of "one holy church" that it "is the assembly of saints in which the Gospel is taught purely and the sacraments are administered rightly," and that "both the sacraments and the Word are effectual by reason of the institution and commandment of Christ even if they are administered by evil men." [42] Father Theodor Seeger has written about the ecumenical features in recent German Protestant and Roman Catholic liturgies. The one most prominent common factor in the major service of both confessions, he finds, is the polarity between Word and sacrament. Any effort to revitalize this service at its biblical sources and in its missionary appeal, Seeger concludes, must show the same bipolar concern for "authentic" proclamation of the word and "distinctively Christian" administration of the sacraments.[43] The church is present, not first where the word and sacraments are *believed,* but where they are being *preached and administered,* and the church which is present in that ministration, in that "communicating of holy things," is the one, holy, catholic and apostolic church.

May I become personal for a moment? If what you and I are saying to one another is the gospel, then the church is present here in her gospel independently of your or my personal relationship to either the gospel or the church. Our conversation is a case, then, of the church's calling to herself. Because Christ is present in his word and because the body is where her head is— "Where I am, there shall my servant be also" (Jn. 12:26) —therefore the whole holy Christianhood converges in such dialogue. Provided that what I am speaking is "the

42. Tappert, *op. cit.,* pp. 32–33.
43. *Wort und Sakrament im Gottesdienst der Konfessionen* (Essen: Ludgerus Verlag, 1963), pp. 256–257.

good and gracious word of God," then in that speaking, irrespective of my own status within the church, it is the church which speaks. How, in short, do we know it is the church? In the same way that we recognize the word as Christ's. How could Justin Martyr, in his apologia before the Roman authorities, speak so confidently in behalf of the universal Christian "we," who had not knowingly authorized his testimony and of whom only a fraction could have been known to him personally, and how could he be sure that "we" in fact embody all the glorious things he claimed for "us"? Answer: "It is Jesus Christ who has taught us these things, having been born for this purpose and crucified under Pontius Pilate. . . ." [44]

Later on, when the end came, Justin and his fellow-martyrs would draw strength—or shall I say "power" or even "authority"?—from their solidarity with this Christian "we." "Do what you want," he finally cried to the prosecutor, "we are Christians"—as though their bond with the "Christians" explained their courage. "We wish to undergo vengeance for the sake of the Lord Jesus Christ and thus be saved." [45] Whom did Justin mean by "we"? Only those martyrs in his pitiful little band? Or all Christians? Probably he meant the former, but he was entitled to mean the latter. He had that authority upon earth. "If they persecuted me," Justin's Master had once said, "they will persecute you. . . . All this they will do to you on my account" (Jn. 15:20, 21). That was why Justin was authorized to die "for the sake of the Lord Jesus Christ." But it was by that very same authority that he could appeal to his association

44. *The First Apology of Justin the Martyr*, ed. and tr. by E. R. Hardy, in *Library of Christian Classics* (Philadelphia: The Westminster Press, 1953), vol. I, p. 249.
45. Werner Elert, tr. by C. V. Schindler, *The Christian Ethos* (Philadelphia: Muhlenberg Press, 1957), p. 354.

with the "Christians," and was right to be encouraged by it.

> Only one person speaks here, but as we hear him we hear them all. He represents the whole, and the whole is his strength and support. He cannot speak for every individual because he cannot vouch for every individual, but he can speak for the community because it is community.[46]

"Resist [the adversary], firm in your faith," an earlier Christian had urged his fellow-martyrs, "knowing that the same experience of suffering is required of your brotherhood throughout the world" (I Pet. 5:9). "If one member suffers, all suffer together; if one member is honored, all rejoice together" (Rom. 12:26).

Similarly, as the Apology to the Augsburg Confession states, those confessors were of course not indifferent either to the discord which threatened or to their own peril. Yet their appeal was not for a right to dissent or even for a right to be heard as a group. Appealing in effect beyond their accusers, to God but also to the whole church, they confidently submitted their claim ("that we hold to the Gospel of Christ correctly and faithfully") to the judgment of Christendom, "all nations" and also "posterity," and thus they waxed bold in the universal company.[47] At the martyrdom of Polycarp, although this dauntless old man stood in the flames alone, the record reports that even the hostile mob saw him as a representative of a community: "the whole crowd marveled that there should be such a difference between the unbelievers and the elect." [48] That association would probably not have surprised Polycarp, for we are told something

46. *Ibid.*, p. 353.
47. Tappert, *op. cit.*, p. 99.
48. *The Martyrdom of Polycarp*, ed. and tr. by M. H. Shepherd, Jr., in *Library of Christian Classics, op. cit.*, p. 155.

about the prayer he prayed in preparation for his burning—". . . his prayer, in which he remembered all who
had met with him at any time, both small and great, both
those with and without renown, and the whole Catholic
Church throughout the world." [49] These examples of the
church's apologists, confessors and martyrs (as of "our
brethren" in the Apocalypse who "loved not their lives
even unto death") are meant to make a point. May they
remind the angelist, for whom the church is admittedly
one but merely "invisibly" one, that the one church not
only is visible—"hidden," as Luther would say, yes, yet
hidden under quite bodily, observable activity—but also
has power upon earth through these very visible em-
bodiments to embolden the dispersed angels of Michael
and to reassure the little flock of its immense connec-
tions.

All this, finally, comes to fruition at the level of grassroots, back-fence ecumenism and in pastoral practice.
What the pastor can do is to assure his flock of that body
whose hands and feet and voices they are. This is not
easy. They may understand well enough that when he,
the pastor, is speaking to them—speaking the gospel to
them—really the whole Christian body is speaking to
them. That they may believe. But what they also have a
right to remember is that when they in turn speak the
words of forgiveness to their spouses, when they feed
their hungry youngsters in the name of Christ, when
they clothe the naked in the community in his name,
they are not doing this on their own and alone but
rather as the agents of the whole embodied Christ, in
behalf of the brotherhood throughout the world. They
may understand well enough, when they sing the *Te
Deum* in public worship, that they are but the voices of
"the glorious company of the apostles, . . . the goodly

49. *Ibid.,* p. 151.

fellowship of the prophets, . . . the noble army of martyrs, . . . the holy church throughout the world." That
they may understand. What they are free to remember
as well, because of the victory of Michael and all of his
angels, is that when they are praising God with their
acts of mercy in their weekday callings, healing all manner of diseases in Christ's name, casting out who-knows-
what-kind of demons in his name, they are not then
suddenly reduced to singing solo. Then and there,
through them, "all the earth doth worship, . . . all angels
cry aloud, the heavens and all the powers therein"—and
"the holy church throughout all the world."

The plainest Christians may understand that, when a
Justin Martyr confessed his faith before his Roman accusers, he was testifying for all of us. That they may
believe. What they are entitled to remember, too, is that
when in their various callings they bear reproach and
absorb the rebuff and shoulder the dear holy cross, they
do so not in isolation but as the shoulders of the body of
Christ, whole and entire. They may understand that,
when I their pastor pronounce the absolution, it is valid
and effectual even if I were a hypocrite and did not
believe it myself. That they may know well enough.
What they are also authorized to know is that when they,
in the world, repay evil with good, even though they do
so with mixed motives or weak faith, they nevertheless
do it, and can do it avidly, as the agents of Christ and of
his holy church. Will their knowing that tempt them to
be hypocrites? Maybe. That, as we said before, is a risk.
But it might also be the thing which will relieve them of
that very self-concern, that preoccupation with their own
fears and the divine criticism and the accusations of the
adversary, which so quickly beget hypocrisy. Knowing
that the work of the church, even her work through me,
does not depend for its value on the purity of my heart—

knowing that may be the very thing which bolsters and purifies my heart. The pastor owes his people this assurance of what cosmic company they keep. But he should also be warned that the practice of such a spirituality, once begun, is not easy to contain. Once Christian people know who all are singing along with them in the Thrice Holy on Sunday morning, ("with angels and archangels and all the company of heaven") once they know who all "our brethren" are who are conquering the accuser "by the blood of the Lamb and by the word of their testimony," they are likely to "rejoice." And only the Lord knows where that can lead.

THE HOLY SPIRIT AND AUTHORITY

by Bernard J. Cooke, S. J.

IN A SUBJECT as vast as the one assigned to us, "The Holy Spirit and Authority," one could obviously treat the topic in many different fashions. There is possible a comparative study of the different communities within Christianity today and their view of the relationship of these two realities. One could make an historical analysis of the way in which, during the past two thousand years, Christianity in its various expressions has dealt with this relationship. What I propose to do in the present paper is to confine myself very largely to the Old and New Testament texts themselves, and to move from this basis into a certain amount of theological reflection. This approach runs a danger of not being a purely exegetical analysis, perhaps of introducing too much of one's own theological presuppositions into a study of the text. However, I think it may serve as a basis for a fruitful interchange of views.

As one approaches the notion of spirit in the Old Testament, one finds no difficulty in discerning several elements of relationship between spirit and authority. A number of authoritative figures in Old Testament times—Moses, the kings and the prophets—are spoken of as being filled with the spirit and being moved by the spirit of Yahweh. Whenever one uses the word "authoritative" of these various individuals one must necessarily adjust the notion as he moves, let us say, from Moses himself to the kings of Israel and then on to the prophets. There is no question but what these individuals do have authority within the society of Israel, but the foundation for their authority is apparently quite different.

Yet, as one examines these various instances of authority figures within the structure of Israel there is a common element that apparently is of considerable importance in our investigation of the Holy Spirit and authority. All of those to whom the spirit is granted are individuals who bear for the sake of Israel the authoritative and life-giving word of Yahweh. In a sense, the authority they possess is not because of themselves as individuals but, if one can put it that way, in terms of their occupying a role within Israel's life. What grants them authority is God's own word which they speak.

Moses of course is seen to be in a unique position in this regard because his word, the word of law, is that which bears the will of Yahweh and necessarily therefore functions to establish and to structure the very roots of Israel's history.

With the kings, one passes into a considerably different situation, for here are men who occupy the supreme position of institutional authority within Israel. Yet even in this instance they are speaking of the law as the guide for the life of the people. They still are radically speaking of the word of Yahweh. It is really quite interesting to notice how little there is of what one might call regal legislation in Old Testament times. The law by which Israel is to be ruled is still essentially the law which came through Moses.

With the prophets a still different situation emerges, for, occupying no particular structural position, at least in the political or sacerdotal situation, these men still exercised a unique guidance of society, a unique authority. This, as we can see from the texts which describe their own prophetic vocation, derives from the word of Yahweh which is given through their lips.

Even such brief reference to these elements from Old Testament times points up the intrinsic relationship between a vocation to speak for Yahweh and the possession of the spirit which moves the individual to speak and makes his words, words of power. Moreover, reflection on these texts indicates that we really must speak of authority in a multiple sense if we are to discuss the relationship of the Holy Spirit and authority accurately. Though the two elements were sometimes found in the same man, as in Moses, one notices already a distinction between what one might call institutional authority and charismatic authority.

There are those who because they function at the top of the institutional structures of the people possess that authority, and those who, because of a special charismatic or prophetic insight, bear the authority of revealed truth. Nor would it be correct to say that only the latter have authority because of the spirit. The history of Israel points to the fact that spirit manifests itself in the institutional translation of their faith as well as in the prophetic oracles. And the dialectic between institutional and charismatic was at times a tension only because either one or other expression of the word and of the spirit tended to be distorted or misunderstood.

Israel's prophets did not speak out essentially against the validity of Old Testament institutional forms. What they denounced was the fact that these forms were lived in infidelity to the deeper faith-insights which were meant to be their heart and of which they were meant to be a societal translation. If the prophets spoke out against the kings and the priests, it was because these latter were not truly working according to the spirit of Yahweh. Yahweh's spirit is not to be found in the excessive legalism discernible at certain times of Old Testament development. Yet anyone who holds to a charismatic origin for the scriptural word of God must admit that in the people's retention of and development of Old Testament law there was present the working of the spirit of God. Thus, both aspects, institutional and charismatic, find their origin in the word of Yahweh and in his spirit.

New Testament literature clearly presents Jesus from the moment of his baptism onward as a Messiah endowed with the Spirit, though now the Spirit begins to be manifested as distinct from the Father and from Jesus. In the baptism scene, as Jesus the new Israel, the new Moses, passes through the waters and into the desert, it is in the power of the Spirit that has been revealed at the moment of the baptism. Again in the scene of the transfiguration it seems that the manifestations of the cloud is to be linked with the Old Testament notion of the *Kebod Yahweh,* with the presence of God's redemptive spirit to his people, and with his presence to the Jerusalem Temple.

Moreover, as one examines carefully the description of Christ's years of public ministry, one sees that the early Church was conscious that the Spirit manifested himself through the external actions of Christ, above all, through the power of his causative speech. Luke tells us in the final verse of his description of the baptism-temptation scene that Christ, having rejected the false spirit, left the desert in the power of the spirit of God. Jesus himself, when accused by the Scribes and Pharisees of doing his wondrous public deed through the power of Beelzebub, charges these critics of blasphem-

ing against the Spirit. This charge indicates his awareness that the spirit in his divine wisdom was the one
who was at the source of Christ's own humanly manifested power. The Old Testament conjunction of the
mysteries of God's word and God's spirit is manifested
now in this man who is Jesus. Christ's words are words of
power and authority. The Greek word *exousia* is constantly utilized to point to Christ's operative authority
over the myster of evil, whether that evil manifested
itself in the ignorance and prejudices and errors of man,
or in the bodily ailments and malformations of people,
or most radically in the mystery of moral evil. To him
who was the Son of Man was given *exousia* even in this
world, the power that made it possible for him to enter
into conflict with the deepest powers of chaos and to
overcome them.

During the days of his public life, though he was already utilizing his authority to lay the foundations for
the Christian community, Christ apparently occupied no
position of institutional authority. He spoke with an assurance which was undeniable, with a prophetic voice
that was clear and striking, and this the people recognized. Essentially, however, one might say that it was
basically a charismatic manifestation which was to be
found in this man Jesus. As a matter of fact, his unique
charismatic insight came into conflict with the closed,
institutionalized patterns of much of the Judaism which
he encountered. And he condemned the inability of
these institutional forms to contain the power of the
Spirit which was working in himself.

Yet, he did seem rather clearly to be pointing to the
fact that that which worked in him in a highly personal-
ized context was meant to find continuation and growth
through the societal forms of a community of faith. This
he did in his promise of societal authority to those who

were his closest disciples and above all to Peter. However, even those inchoate authority patterns remain only in a potential state until the Spirit is breathed into them with the mystery of Pentecost.

Authority, both charismatic and institutional, as an actual operative mystery of Christian community, finds its focus in the mystery of the risen Lord himself. With his own resurrection, Christ enters completely into the mystery of life dominated by spirit, so that, as Paul tells us, he becomes himself life-giving spirit. This seems not only concomitant but intrinsically bound up with his role as the Lord of the Christian community and the Lord of human history. It is as the Lord, with the full authority of the Son of man come into glory, that he is enabled to send his Spirit into that community which is to be his historical continuation and fulfillment.

This is not to say that he hands over to this new people of God the charismatic authority and the institutional authority which are his. Rather the Church is the mystery of his remaining as Lord in the midst of this community, present to them by the very fact that he constantly imparts to them his spirit. This Spirit is the animating principle of the community, at the root of the authority exercised both in institutional patterns and in charismatic gifts.

As we trace the faith-witness of the primitive community to this process, we see that it begins on the night of Easter itself when in an appearance to his disciples Jesus gives them his Spirit, so that they have authority over the deepest reaches of the mystery of evil—over sin itself. This post-resurrection transmission of his own Spirit to his followers finds its culmination in Pentecost. Here the Spirit is poured out in abundance as Peter's sermon indicates, poured out particularly upon the twelve, though not limited to them. It is in virtue of the Spirit that Peter can now with authority speak to the Jewish people that word which clarifies their own historical role and which points to the realization of Israel and the establishment of the new people of God.

Throughout these early decades, as the Acts of the Apostles indicates, the Spirit worked in very observable fashion in the midst of the newly established community, working in an intertwined process of institutional and charismatic authority. One cannot avoid the impression that the Apostles who had been the pivotal witnesses to the saving event of Christ's passover occupied a position within the community which was normative of the Christian faith-response to Christ. At the same time there was a diversity of gifts coming from the Spirit, so that others interacted with the incipient institutional leaders to convey an understanding of how the community should express its self-identity in the forms of life which it established. If anything is clear from the testimony of the Acts, it is that the Christian community as it emerged out of the Passover mystery, is essentially a community formed by the presence of the indwelling spirit sent into the Church by the Risen Christ.

Intertwined as they are, and oftentimes found in the same persons—for the Apostles clearly possessed charismatic gifts—one can still notice a distinction between what one might call the institutional and charismatic aspects of authority in the primitive Christian community. While they recognize the validity of the charismatic manifestations of the Spirit in many of the early Christians, even in the newly converted, the Apostles were also quite clear that they somehow possessed a normative function with regard to judging the validity and implementation of these charisma. And this role of the Apostles in judging these charismatic utterances by their own historical witness to the realities of Christ's life, death and resurrection was apparently recognized by the community, and accepted as a more ultimate expression of the Spirit in their midst.

Already in the earliest days of the Church there appears a certain dialectic, even a tension, between the two kinds of authority. Those possessing one or the other feel themselves to be genuine manifestations of the Spirit. Both feel that somehow Christ himself is exercising his authority as Lord and Messiah through the gifts of the Spirit which they possess and which they attempt to apply to the developing life of the Christian Church. Yet somehow the role of the Twelve as the guides of faith seems to be a dominant note beginning with the mystery of Pentecost itself. As we read in the second chapter of Acts, the primitive Christian community, following the event of the descent of the Spirit, formed by this pouring out of God's Spirit, assembled together to have its new life shaped by the apostolic instruction. Apparently, even that great charismatic figure, Paul, felt the need to compare his own insights with the historical experience and witness of Peter.

It might be well at this point to turn our attention to an allied aspect of both Old and New Testament development, the origin of the sacred literature. If one takes seriously the faith of both communities, Israel and Christianity, one must attribute to Sacred Scripture a certain charismatic origin rooted essentially in the prophetic insight into history possessed by men like the prophets or the Apostles. The Scriptures are the specially guided expression of a charismatic community's encounter with the revealing God.

It seems that the faith-community, under this special guidance of the Spirit of God, felt the need to preserve and finally gather together an expression of its faith. This could act as a norm of judgment for future faith insight and charismatic experience. When one seeks the ultimate norm of judging between the true and the false prophet in Israel, it seems to be essentially in fidelity to the covenant traditions of the people. When in later times the Scripture became a settled body of religious tradition, it was utilized to judge and form, not just the external expressions of Israelite life, but also the inner life of the spirit in Israel. As one studies the use of Scripture in the religious ceremonial of the later Old Testament centuries, one can see that the institutional authority itself was partially responsible for this normative function of Scripture. Faithful to its own genius, the priesthood utilized the Scripture as an essential means of exercising its own proper authority. Thus there is an interplay between the institutional authority present in the faith community and the authority exercised by Scripture as the expression of the faith community's charismatic insights into sacred history.

In New Testament times, the pattern is essentially the same. Scripture emerges out of the apostolic explanation of the mystery of Christ, and to a very considerable extent is produced by the liturgical catechesis of the infant Church. The New Testament Scriptures, written as they are under special direction of the Spirit in the community, come to possess authority as a norm for faith. Charismatic in origin, Scripture becomes an integral part of the institutionalized stabilization of faith and an unparralleled instrument of the authoritative teaching group within the Christian community.

Being the product both of charismatic and institutional processes, the Scriptures were, from their beginning, open to interpretation by both the institutional and charismatic elements within the Christian community. This is clearly manifested in the deep religious questions which ante-dated and helped to bring about the conflict of Reformation times. This conflict was not exactly one of opposing Scripture and tradition. Rather the conflict dealt with the way one reads Scripture, the respective roles within the Christian community of authoritative teachers and of charismatic religious figures relative to understanding the Scriptural word of God. Actually, Scripture must itself act as norm for both charismatic understanding and institutional life. In turn, Scripture is translated and expressed in form contemporary with each human generation both by the institutional patterns of Christian community and by the charismatic insights of those related in special familiarity to the mystery of God.

One asks, then, whether one is faced with an unavoidable historical conflict and antimony between the charismatic and the institutional. Each unquestionably has an authority proper to itself, each has an authority to speak for God to all who will hear the Gospel and receive it in faith. As one examines the New Testament literature, one sees a possible point of resolution. This is Christian charity.

There is only one spirit in the Church, just as there is only one Lord. Ultimately this spirit cannot be working at odds with himself in the two manifestations of which we have spoken. Since He is the Spirit of love, it is in this area that we might find some resolution of the problem which we have raised.

Paul tells us in I Corinthians that of all the gifts of the Spirit the most important, the most precious, and the most lasting, is the gift of the love of Christ. All other things will pass, but this charism will remain as the very heart of the Spirit's operation in the mystery of Christ. In its own way it acts as a judge on all the other charismatic gifts: if they do not lead to a deepened love of Christians among themselves and of the Christian com-

munity for Christ, they are an illusion and not to be
trusted. At the same time, Christian love is the key to
all societal authority possessed within the Christian
community. This one reality, Christ's love abiding in the
community, is in the last analysis the root reality behind
all authority, be it charismatic or institutional.

Perhaps some exploration of the way in which love is
the key to genuine societal authority within Christianity
might be in order. Actually, the New Testament texts
that can be marshalled in this regard leave us with a
very clear-cut conclusion. When speaking to his disciples
on the occasion of their disputes as to who would occupy
the positions of honor within the kingdom, Christ clarifies for them the nature of his own authority which, as
we have seen, is the only ultimate abiding authority
within the Church. Not as among the Gentile rulers is
authority to be served. He will give his life, not just as
something juxtaposed to the exercise of authority but as
a very means of exercising his authority.

When in Luke's Gospel the scene is transposed into
the situation of the Cenacle, we can see that the exercise
of authority is somehow intrinsically linked with the
Eucharistic mystery. It centers around Christ's life-giving act of communicating himself, the source of life,
to those who are his followers. It seems rather clear that
Christ who gives a kingdom to his disciples in order that
they may eat and drink at his table, is telling these
disciples that they must do as he has done—minister to
those who are their charge by the gift of themselves, their
faith, their love, their persons, their very life if it should
be required. Only in this way will they deeply rule the
hearts and minds of men, by winning their love and
leading them to share the goals and faith which are
their own. The impression gleaned from these texts is
deepened as one examines the teaching of the Fifth

Chapter of *Ephesians*. This is part of a moral catechesis describing for the Christian community what is to be their attitude toward the patterns of societal authority. Discussing the situation of the family, *Ephesians* points out that Christian husbands are to love their wives as Christ loved the Church and gave himself up for her. We can see then the authority-role of Christ with regard to the Christian community described profoundly in terms of a loving gift of self, so that the other might live and be perfected. Intrinsically linked as it is with the whole mystery of human married love, the authority of the Church can have meaning only in terms of this kind of loving self-gift.

Rapid and most inadequate as this analysis has been, I think it does point to the fact that the early Christian community saw the exercise of societal authority as being very profoundly a mystery of Christian love rather than any type of civil exercise of dominating authority. The Spirit of charity, Christ's own Spirit, is the root therefore of any institutional manifestation of Christ's rule.

To guarantee the retention of that perspective, the Spirit has worked throughout the centuries of the Church's life through charismatic individuals who act as a constant reminder that the societal patterns of the Church may never crystallize into a meaningless legalism or into a narrowness which will deny the free working of the Spirit. The charismatic in the Christian community, if it be genuine, must in itself be an expression of love which respects the integrity and identity of a continuing mystery of the Church. It must see in the faith-community and its valid institutional forms, a reality which is also an expression of the spirit, an expression which in the last analysis is normative even of its own reality.

The Spirit, then, stands at the origin of all authority within the Christian community, but it is so as sent from Christ who is the head of the Body and the Lord of the new people. Because he imparts life to the very institutional structures of this faith-community, the Spirit is the origin of whatever power is exercised by those occupying authoritative institutional positions. Yet he also is the one who in speaking through the genuinely charismatic figures gives them the authority which they have because of their prophetic insight. Thirdly, he manifests himself in and through the written word of Scripture which has a special authoritative function precisely because it is not simply the word of man but, in the midst of the Christian community, the constantly imparted word of God. Any conflict between authority and the Spirit can only be apparent and due to our human misunderstandings of either or both realities.

WORSHIP

THE HOLY SPIRIT IN RUSSIAN-ORTHODOX DEVOTIONAL LIFE

by Helene Iswolsky *

Author's Note: This is a study of the devotional aspect of the Russian-Orthodox conception of the Holy Spirit in Christian life both in the social and in the individual dimension, in the human person's soul and in the community. Since this conception is based on Eastern theology from patristic times up to the nineteenth and twentieth centuries, the paper had, of course to deal also with the theological aspect. The author, however, did not attempt to present a complete theology of the Paraclete as it is developed by the Eastern Church, nor has a detailed Ecclesiology of the East been defined, this not being the topic of the present study. Only the main points of both theology and ecclesiology have been brought out, in relation to Russian-Orthodox private and public devotion to the Paraclete. These points are given according to the opinion of Russian-Orthodox and Catholic theologians who are authorities on the subject, even if their opinions differ or conflict on certain points. In speaking of the Western liturgy, the

* Helene Iswolsky (Byzantine Catholic) is Professor of Russian Literature, Seton Hill College. She is the author of *Christ in Russia* and the editor of *The Third Hour*. She is also an associate editor of the *Journal of Ecumenical Studies*.

author has used the word *Roman* rather than *Latin* since the use of the vernacular in most of the Mass and parts of the Office seems to require a new terminology. The paper deals with the Russian-Orthodox devotion to the Holy Spirit, which in many ways, of course, is similar to the Greek Orthodox conception and to the Slavonic one in other countries where this rite is observed; however, the Russian-Orthodox have developed this theme in their own characteristic way, especially after Alexey Khomyakov's ecclesiology. The liturgies of Eastern Churches united to Rome follow the same pattern.

The theme of the Russian people's devotion to the Holy Spirit is one of the most attractive ones in Eastern religious studies because of the important part played by the Paraclete in the entire economy of Russian spiritual life.

The Byzantine liturgy in its Slavonic version is, as it has often been said, a resplendent icon, or rather a *triptych*, illustrating the Triune God, the Church invisible in theology and in Community life. In this liturgy, the Holy Spirit is continually invoked, either together with the other persons of the Trinity, or separately, as the life-giver, the Divine breath, the *pneuma* energizing and transfiguring the human soul in the image of the Creator.

The liturgy, however, is not the only projection of the Holy Spirit's presence among the faithful. The great Russian-Orthodox theologian, Alexis Khomyakov, wrote: "The Holy Church confesses her faith in her entire life: in her teaching, which is inspired by the Holy Spirit, in the Sacraments, in which the Holy Spirit is active and in the rites which He also governs." [1] To this activity, as we might say, within the Temple, we must add the

1. A. Khomyakov. *Tserkov Odna* (New York, 1955), p. 214.

people's devotional life outside the magisterium and the rites, either as an entire social and ethical conception (justice, charity, freedom in human relations), or a spiritual way, a method of prayer and contemplation ("the acquisition of the Holy Spirit," taught by St. Seraphim of Sarov), or again a certain emphasis in private prayer and devotions on the role of the Parclete in spiritual enlightenment.

This emphasis, to which we shall often refer in our analysis of both public or private devotions, is not, however, an "overemphasis" as some uninformed writers seem to think. The accumulation of texts, translated from Russian-Orthodox religious thinkers, without sufficient analysis or understanding of linguistic subtleties, may be misleading inasmuch as they present only one part of the *triptych;* such a division between the Three Persons actually never occurs. Even Father Sergius Bulgakov, who is considered one of the most advanced contemporary Russian-Orthodox theologians, speaks of worship as the contemplation of the Incarnation *and* Pentecost.

Vladimir Lossky, the young theologian who succeeded Bulgakov, clearly defined this parallel between the Incarnation and Pentecost in his treatise on the "Mystical Theology of the Eastern Church." [2] According to Lossky, Christ, the Incarnate Word, deifies (transfigures) human nature as a whole, the Holy Spirit deifies each human person separately.[3]

The doctrine of *deification* which is one of the central themes of Orthodox mystical theology does certainly rely a great deal on the action of the Holy Spirit. In his book *The Orthodox Church* Timothy Ware describes this ac-

2. Vladimir Lossky *Essai sur la Theologie Mystique de l'Eglise d'Orient* (Paris, 1944).

3. See also the article of D. E. Lanne, "Le Mystere de l'Eglise dans la Perspective de la Theologie Orthodoxe," *Irenikon* No. 2 (1962), pp. 170–212.

tion, pointing out at the same time that deification is not the work of the Paraclete alone, but "of the Trinitarian God." He writes:

> Behind the doctrine of deification there lies the idea of man made according to the image and likeness of God the Holy Trinity. "May they all be one," Christ prayed at the Last Supper; "as Thou Father, art in me and I in Thee, so also may they dwell in us (John 27:21)." Just as the three persons of the Trinity "dwell in one another" in an unceasing movement of love, so man made in the image of the Trinity is called to "dwell" in the Trinitarian God. . . . The saints, as Maximus the Confessor put it, are those who express the Holy Trinity in themselves.[4]

The Russian-Orthodox theologian, Father George Florovsky, one of the greatest living authorities on Orthodox doctrine disagrees with V. Lossky; he does not conceive the action of the Holy Spirit as differentiated from that of the Incarnation. In his opinion, the "Economy" of Christ and of the Paraclete cannot be separated; they are not only parallel, but intimately bound together. The Church is essentially the body of Christ on which Orthodox ecclesiology is founded.

Having made this assertion, Father Florovsky's conception of the *Ecclesia* is still inspired by the Christological and Pentecostal aspect, which though bound together, continue to represent two poles around which worship is centered: "The life of the Church is founded on two correlative mysteries," he writes, "the mystery of the Holy Supper and the Mystery of Pentecost. This duality will be found everywhere in the life of the Church." [5]

4. Timothy Ware, *The Orthodox Church* (Baltimore, 1963), p. 236.
5. George Florovsky, *Puty Russkogo Bogoslovya* (Paris, 1937), quoted by Lanne, p. 180.

In order to grasp the full meaning of this life of the Church both in Christ and in the Holy Spirit, we must recall that the Christian East has been, generally speaking, as Father Yves Congar puts it, "spontaneously and intimately Platonic since patristic days. The present world is for her an epiphany of the spiritual world and refers to it not only in its finality and extrinsic order, but by its interior substance and its very reality." [6]

The Platonic interpretation of the world found in the Church is further developed in Christian life which is, as we have seen, understood in Orthodox mystical theology, as *deification*. The young Russian-Orthodox theologian, Father John Meyendorff, writing on this subject reminds us of the statement by St. Athanasius of Alexandria: "God became man that we may become God (The Incarnation of the Word)." Deification, Father Meyendorff explains, is achieved by becoming part of the Body of Christ, but especially through "the economy" of the Paraclete. And he concludes, quoting from the epistle to the Galatians: "God has sent out the Spirit of his Son, crying out in us 'Abba, Father'" (4:6). [7]

One may say that Russian-Orthodox theology of our days is returning more and more to patristic doctrine as well as to the Scriptures. Contemporary Russian theologians are careful not to make any overstatement concerning the pneumatological aspect of the Church and of Christian life. Nevertheless, they continue to be profoundly aware of the Pentecostal mystery, without which the ecclesiological and liturgical triptych would not have attained its fullness.

This is why, in spite of certain reservations, and even criticisms expressed by contemporary Russian theolog-

---

6. Yves Congar, O.P., *Chrétiens Desunis* (Paris, 1937), p. 252.
7. John Meyendorff, *The Orthodox Church* (New York, 1962), pp. 195–6.

ical thought, the writings of the Slavophile religious leaders, Alexis Khomyakov and the brothers Kireyevsky, continue to inform certain deep, and, one might say, perennial undercurrents of the Russians' devotion to Pentecost. For ever since Orthodox religious thought was revitalized a century ago by Khomyakov's "The Church is one," there has been a strong and convincing appeal in his words:

> The Church lives even on Earth not a human, but a divine life, a life of Grace. Her visible manifestation is continued in the Sacraments; her interior life—in the gifts of the Holy Spirit, in Faith, Hope and Charity. . . . She lives not under the laws of slavery, but under the law of freedom, recognizes no authority except her own, no judgement except the judgement of Faith (for reason cannot grasp her) and expresses her charity in prayers and rites, which the Spirit of Truth and the Grace of God inspire her with. This is why the very rites, though not invariable (for they are created by the Spirit of freedom and may be altered by the decision of the Church), can never and in no way contain the slightest admixture of lies or false doctrine. As to the rites which have not been changed by the Church, they are compulsory for the members of the Church, for their observance is the joy of holy unity.[8]

In these words we find the key to the very meaning of the liturgy in the eyes of the Russian-Orthodox. The rites are not only an Icon, or triptych created by man, they are given to us by the Spirit of Truth. It has often been said that the Byzantine liturgy is a Theophany; it is also a theology, and in a certain sense—a charisma.

Yves Congar grasped the profound meaning of the Orthodox cult when he wrote:

---

8. S. Bulgakov, *Orthodoxie* (Paris, 1932), p. 5.

Although in the West the word "rite" is taken in the narrow sense, it is understood in a broader and deeper sense in the East. This brings about a type of piety that is very simple and yet very deep, not analytically developed in logical deductions and practical applications, but continually vitalized in the services of the Church, a type of piety in which the meanings of the rite, the faith and the Church are united in a single living attitude.[9]

In his treatise "The Church is One," as well as in his other writings, Khomyakov reinstated the continuity of the Church as primarily postulated in Eastern ecclesiology. Commenting upon this concept of continuity, Father Bernard Lambert, O.P., explains it by the Castern Church's "unchanged recognition of Jesus Christ as the only Head of the Church; faith and love, as the only poles of the ecclesiastical life and of the liturgy through which the faithful take possession of the very power of the Resurrected Christ." [10]

That the liturgy exercises not only dogmatic authority, but also a powerful spiritual action was strongly felt by the Russian writer Nicholas Gogol. In his remarkable treatise "Meditations on the Divine Liturgy," Gogol wrote:

> Great and innumerable would be the effects of the divine liturgy, if man listened to it in order to bring it into his life. Teaching all equally, acting equally along all the links of the chain, from the tsar to the last beggar, it speaks to all of the same things, though not in the same way, it teaches all love, which is the uniting

9. Yves Congar, O.P., *After One Hundred Years* (New York, 1959), p. 36.
10. Bernard Lambert, O.P., *Le Probleme Oecumenique* (Paris 1961).

link of society, the secret spring of all that moves, the food, the life of all.[11]

To this essential conception of the Church unchanged throughout the ages, Alexey Khomyakov brought, so to say, a new dimension; he turned more specially his attention on that third panel of the divine triptych, on the freedom of the Spirit which blows where *he will* and distributes his gifts as *he wills;* the Spirit which grants man his free choice, till he finds his salvation not so much through the image of the crucified as of the resurrected, glorified Christ, and of the Pentecost which followed his glorification.

The conception was further developed and widened by Khomyakov's followers. They considered that the West had made of the Church an organization instead of the organic entity which it was in the days of the Apostles. The Church of Christ according to Father Sergius Bulga-kov, is not an institution, but a new life in Christ, directed by the Holy Spirit.

Khomyakov went so far as to deny the Church any magisterium properly speaking; in his mind, ecumenical councils themselves are a manifestation of faith, not a dogmatic authority. We have already seen that contemporary Russian-Orthodox theologians are in disagreement with the Slavophile leaders in certain of their extreme points. Their exact positions should be defined before the question of authority in Orthodox ecclesiology can be fully discussed or even opened to discussion. Since this paper is concerned with the devotion of the Russian-Orthodox to the Holy Spirit rather than with pneumatological theology, we have largely sought to bring out the main aspects of this theology as reflected

11. Nicholas Gogol, *Razmyshleniya o Bozhestvennoy Liturgiy.*

in the liturgy as well as in Russian religious and social thought.

We have seen that the two poles, Christ and the Holy Spirit, inform and energize the Russian's religious experience. It has developed in the light of Resurrection (Christ) and in the pentecostal fire descended on the apostles. They are the Church and will draw all the faithful to this Church united in charity. The Body of Christ is also the unity of all the faithful, both hierarchy, priesthood and laity filled with the love which is the gift of the Holy Spirit.[12] This is the central idea of Russian-Orthodoxy, the idea of *SOBORNOST*, a word which is untranslatable in any other language. It means a mystical assembly, a spiritual council, a community and a communion of persons held together by a spiritual bond, yet preserving the fullness of their individual freedom. It is not an institution, as Sergius Bulgakov said, but an organic whole.

We know how deeply Dostoyevsky penetrated the problem of spiritual freedom (the Grand Inquisitor) as the supreme gift received from Christ and which atheist utopians would take away from him. "Dostoyevsky was a child of Orthodoxy," writes Father De Lubac. "Theologians of his own country may not have been wholly satisfied as to the correctness of his beliefs, but it would be risking a grave mistake in the interpretation of his work to forget that he breathed the atmosphere of Orthodoxy." [13]

And this is true of other Russian writers and religious thinkers. It is true, of course, of Berdyaev, who cannot

12. In Russian-Orthodox terminology charity is not a theological virtue, but a gift of the Holy Spirit.
13. Henri De Lubac, S.J., *The Drama of Atheist Humanism* (New York 1950), p. 237.

be considered a classic Russian Orthodox philosopher, but whose very idea of freedom as an essentially Christian virtue, incompatible with materialism, breathes that peculiar "atmosphere" of Russian mystical theology. No wonder then that Berdyaev could write so profoundly about Dostoyevsky's concept of freedom as a supernatural category opposed to the natural, and therefore restricted and sterile, manifestations of man's self-will.

> Every man is offered the alternative of the Grand Inquisitor or of Jesus Christ and he must accept one or the other, for there is no third choice. In the Grand Inquisitor's system self-will leads to the negation and loss of freedom of spirit which can be found again in Christ alone.[14]

These are indeed forceful words elevating the quality of freedom to supernatural dimensions. But where, it might be asked, is the breath of the Holy Spirit found in Berdyaev? We shall answer, nowhere and everywhere. For it is precisely characteristic of Russian-Orthodox thought not to make any over-statements regarding the separate role of each person of the Holy Trinity. The only Russian writer who sought to be a religious thinker exclusively promoting the Holy Spirit was Dimitry Merezhkovsky. This gifted and inspired author had been one of the initiators of the Russian religious revival which marked the decades preceding the revolution. He was at that time, together with his wife, the poetess Zinaida Hippius, the leading spirit of the Religious-Philosophical Society of Petersburg which had as one of its aims the struggle against the spread of atheism among the Russian intellectual elite. Later, Merezhkovsky drifted away from the strictly Orthodox elements of this

14. Nicholas Bedyaev, *Dostoevsky* (New York, 1964), p. 188.

society. He created his own religion, the "cult of the Holy Spirit," whose advent was, in his mind so imminent, that all previous theologizing should be cancelled, as well as all formal liturgical traditions. This theory, though brilliantly presented by the Merezhkovskys and a small group of followers, failed to attract wide interest and practically vanished after the death of its initiators.

It should be recalled, however, that a special cult of the Holy Spirit was observed by certain Russian religious sects which had completely broken with Orthodoxy and whose practices were condemned not only as heretical, but immoral. Thus for instance the Khylysty, whose vigils turned into orgies, and whose "prophetesses" or "Mothers of God" reigned over congregations known as "ships," based their teaching on the so-called "Book of the Dove," and their emblem was a "silver dove." [15] Their cults present considerable interest for historians of Russian sects, but are not characteristic of Russian devotional life as a whole; they are the remnants of obscure pagan practices and superstitions.

Other groups, like the Dukhobors (Wrestlers by the Spirit), the Molokans, Stundists, etc., which appeared in Russia in the seventeenth and eighteenth centuries and spread in the nineteeth, have little connection, or none with the Silver Dove of the Khylysty. Their teaching is related to what is roughly known as "Spiritual Christianity" of Western Protestant origin, to Illuminism, etc. These sects do have a teaching based on the Holy Spirit, and on the Pauline text concerning men being the "Temples of the Living God" (2 Cor.: 6,16), but this teaching of enlightenment through the Holy Spirit, being common both to East and West, does not necessarily imply any link with Russian popular devotion. On the

15. The symbolist poet, Andrey Biely described this sect in his novel, *The Silver Dove* (Moscow-Petersburg, 1910).

contrary, it appeared rather as a protest against the Russian-Orthodox Church, her dogma, hierarchical structure and liturgical worship.

Nevertheless, certain elements of the Russian forms of Spiritual Christianity must have, no doubt, developed because of the Russian people's attraction to the manifestation of the Holy Spirit in the life of the human person and of society; an indwelling and purifying action for the individual, a bond of unity in mutual love and solidarity for society. It is typical that these Russian sects have a strong attachment to community life, to non-violence, pacifism, and other forms of Christian anarchism, so characteristic of the Russian people's religious ideas, and which, as we know, awakened Tolstoy's interest and sympathy in his dealing with the Dukhobors. A complete study of Russian sects and of their relations both to Western Christianity and to the native religious mind has as yet not been made.[16]

Even so, it can be said that the devotion to the Holy Spirit among a people of Orthodox formation rarely tends toward a particular and strongly emphasized cult. It is the Trinitarian image, the threefold icon which best expresses this devotion. And this economy of the Three Persons is precisely illustrated in Russia's most famous religious painting: the Icon of the Holy Trinity by Andrey Rublev (early fifteenth century).

Rublev's "Trinity" is a symbolic painting, representing the biblical scene of the three strangers visiting Abraham and partaking of a meal under the Terebinths of Mamre. This is a prefiguration of the Eucharistic banquet. The theme taken from Genesis 18:1–10 was often used by both Greek and Russian icon-painters, but

16. For a general survey of Russian sects see Paul Milyukov, *Outlines of Russian Culture*, vol. I (Philadelphia, 1942).

it was Andrey Rublev, a monk of the Monastery of the Trinity and St. Sergius, near Moscow, who rendered the story of this mystic meal with the greatest mastery and with incomparable depth of meaning. Indeed, this icon inspires contemplation, the gradual penetration of Trinitarian theology and its role in the history of salvation. The grace of the three Divine persons, represented as winged angels seems to proclaim the harmony and the economy of the Godhead. At the same time, we feel almost puzzled by the fact that those three figures are identical in face, stature, dress, except for a few details. The question has been often discussed among art-critics and liturgists *which* of the three "strangers" is Christ, and *who* are the two other Persons around the table on which the food has been placed in a vessel resembling a chalice. Opinions have differed; some believe that it is the figure *on the right* of the painting who symbolizes Christ, because the angel's head is slightly drooping and his eyes are fixed on the chalice which some day is to contain his body and blood for the faithful. Others have said that Christ is represented in the central figure, because of the extraordinary gentleness of his expression, but it may be also the third figure, on the left hand side, for a number of other, no less convincing, reasons.

But to leave things unsaid is precisely the aim of this mystic scene, where no rationalization is possible. Dr. A. Avinov, the late curator of Carnegie Museum of Pittsburgh, who was Russian born and who was a great lover of icon-painting, described Rublev's Trinity bringing out its philosophy, or rather, its theology, without seeking to solve the riddle of the identity of the three figures. He stressed instead the supernatural quality of the meal, by saying: "The phantom form of a cup emerging here adumbrates the chalice of the Last Supper and the Eucharist, as though that symbol were lifted into a celestial world above the turbulence and impermanence of things on this earth." [17]

If such then was the fruit of Rublev's contemplation of the persons of the Trinity, the Holy Spirit occupies in his masterpiece a place equal to that of the two other Persons of the Trinity, "indivisible and of one substance," according to the Byzantine liturgy," of "a single nature" according to the Roman-Catholic Mass. Any "special devotion" to the Holy Spirit "would lead to the spiritualism of the Dukhobors and other similar sects, or to Dimitry Merezhkovsky's fanciful pneumatology outside the Trinitarian life. Russian-Orthodox devotion, both private and public, has avoided these deviations and has never broken the continuity of Divine worship.

It is, perhaps, incorrect to speak of the "private devotions" of the Russian-Orthodox. Not because they lack individualism and do not know personal religious experience. As we shall see, the teaching of Saint Seraphim on "the acquisition of the Holy Spirit" is the fruit of an intense religious experience of one man. Nevertheless, it is in the *common* worship of the Church, in her liturgical cycle, in the propers of the Feasts and in the diurnal office that the Russian-Orthodox faithful learn to honor the Holy Spirit and discover his theology. The private prayers addressed to the Paraclete by these faithful in their own homes, and by the hermits in their cells, are the very prayers used in liturgical services. The invocation continually repeated during the daily office, is also a private morning prayer, and is recited by the teacher and the students in class at the beginning of each

17. A. Avinov, *The Russian Icon, its History and Characteristics.*

period (this prayer was said in Russia before the Communist regime suppressed all religious manifestations, and is used by Russian students in private schools outside the USSR.):

> O heavenly King, the Comforter, Spirit of Truth, who art in all places and fillest all things; Treasury of good things and Giver of life: come and take up thine abode in us, and cleanse us from every stain; and save our souls, O Good One.[18]

We see that the Holy Spirit is not invoked by name, but called Heavenly King and omnipresent as are also God the Father and God the Son. But all that follows illustrates, of course, the special operations of the Holy Spirit, or that which is more intimately linked with Him. This prayer is considerably shorter than the *Come Holy Spirit* of the Roman liturgy, and does not have the wealth of epithets and definitions which render the Western prayer so inspiring and poetic. But the Eastern invocation is powerful and convincing even in its brevity; it is made for frequent use and is actually repeated many times a day in the public prayer of the Church or by the faithful in private. It projects very clearly the activity of the *Pneuma* in the Christian and in the Church: the indwelling of the Paraclete, the wealth (treasury) of Gifts, the cleansing power and the life-giving energies and participation in the work of salvation.

The Holy Spirit is separately called upon in the prayers to the Holy Trinity. In the Trisagion in which He is invoked as "Immortal" and in the prayer so often repeated in the liturgy and in private:

18. The translation of this prayer and of all others which follow are from the *Service Book of the Holy Orthodox Apostolic Church*, translated by I. F. Hapgood (Brooklyn, 1956).

O All-Holy Trinity, have mercy on us,
O Lord, wash away our sins,
Master, pardon our transgressions,
O Holy One, visit and heal our infirmities, for thy
name's sake.

The most important role played by the Holy Spirit in
the Russian-Orthodox liturgy is during the Eucharistic
Sacrifice. In the part of the mass known as CONSECRA-
TION, the *canon* of the Byzantine liturgy is similar to
the Roman, almost word for word (except for the
Preface), and is concluded during elevation by the
words of Christ: *"Take, eat, this is my body, which is
broken for you for the remission of sins. Drink ye all of
this; for this is my Blood of the New Testament which is
shed for you and for many, for the remission of sins."*
But these words which commemorate the institution of
the Eucharist are followed in the Byzantine liturgy by
the priest's *silent* prayer known as the *Epiclesis*.

O Lord who at the Third Hour didst send down upon
thine Apostles thy Holy Spirit: take not the same from
us, O Good One, but renew in us who make our
supplication unto thee.

While the priest recites the prayer silently, the choir
sings the hymn:

We sing to Thee. We bless Thee, we thank Thee, we
pray Thee, O God.

During this hymn, the faithful kneel devoutly; though
the prayer of the celebrant is not heard by them, they
know that, according to Orthodox teaching, the moment
of consecration, of *transmutation* (as it is called in
Orthodox terminology rather than transubstantiation)

takes place during the *Epiclesis,* that is *after* the institutional words.

For everyone attending an Orthodox service it is obvious that this is indeed the most solemn moment, for the congregation remains kneeling to the end of the hymn, which also marks the conclusion of the consecration. This is less obvious when the liturgy is performed in a Church of Byzantine rite united to Rome. In this case, the *Epiclesis* does not convey the same crucial meaning as in the Orthodox rite, but still retains its solemnity.

In his "Meditation on the Divine Liturgy" Gogol describes the *Epiclesis* with great pathos:

> After the invocation to the Holy Spirit the Body of Christ lies on the altar. Not an image, not a symbol, but that very body which suffered on Earth, was spat upon and crucified, buried, rose from the dead, ascended to heaven and now sits at the right hand of the Father. It preserves the form of bread only in order to be eaten by man and because Our Lord Himself said: *I am the bread.* The ringing of bells on the church tower announces to all the solemn moment, so that men, wherever they are, on the road, in the fields, at home, or occupied with another task, or on a sick bed, or in prison, might also let their prayer rise at that fearsome instant.[19]

These words could also be said, of course, of the Roman mass, or of any Eucharistic invocation, but Gogol brings out very clearly not the moment of consecration, when the words of institution are said, but precisely the *"fearsome instant"* of the *Epiclesis.*

It is the task of the theologian to explain this difference between the Orthodox and the Roman mass. The Orthodox contend that the *Epiclesis* which existed also in the Latin mass, was dropped in the West in the early

19. N. Gogol, *Razmyshleniya o Bozhestvennoy Liturgiy.*

Middle Ages. This, according to Father John Meyendorff, is held to be a serious defect. The Spirit revealed the mystery of Redemption: "When the lifegiving Spirit, who preceeds from the Father has come to befriend you, he whom I will send to you from the Father's side, he will bear witness of what I was" (John 25:26).

During the last decades, some Russian-Orthodox have adopted in Western countries the mass of the Roman rite as more suitable, it is believed, for non-Greek or non-Slavic faithful converted to Orthodoxy. The Roman-Orthodox rite is actually similar to the Roman-Catholic rite and has several parishes in Europe under the jurisdiction of a Bishop. The Roman mass in these parishes is celebrated in its integrity, but the ancient *Epiclesis* which was dropped in the Middle Ages has been restored. This is the only change required; it proves that the *Epiclesis* is not considered merely a rite, which may or may not be observed, but an essential part of the Eucharistic sacrifice.

If the Divine liturgy invokes the Holy Spirit in a secret prayer, and not aloud for the faithful to hear, the chanting of the hymn "To Thee we sing," marks, as we have seen, for all those attending mass, "the fearsome moment" of the *metabole*. The Russian-Orthodox liturgical prayers do not only illustrate the mysteries but offer a theology and a theophany. This is why the culminating point of the devotion to the Holy Spirit, Pentecost, is one of the greatest feasts of the Russian-Orthodox liturgical cycle. Just as in the Western Church, it is celebrated on the fiftieth day after Easter.

To be more exact, the Holy Spirit is honored not on the Sunday, (tenth day after Ascension) which according to the Orthodox calendar is Trinity Sunday, but on the Monday immediately following it. In fact the Trinity and the "day of the Holy Spirit," as it is called, form one, almost continuous celebration, starting with the vigil of the Feast of the Holy Trinity and ending with the vespers of *Dukhov Denj* (the Day of the Spirit).

In popular devotion, the Feast of the Holy Trinity and *Dukhov Denj* are very colorful and are marked by great rejoicings. This is not the joy of Easter, which climaxes the long period of preparation, the fast and mortification of Lent and Holy Week. It is the continuation of this triumphant feast, the fulfillment of Christ's promise: the indwelling of the Triune God in the souls of the faithful, the descent of the Paraclete on the Church of the Apostles.

Whitsuntide, the feast of new beginnings and of the new man, is also, *par excellence*, the feast of spring, which in Northern countries, is more than anywhere else the propitious season. The long Russian winter, which may have still lent its chill to Easter, especially if it is an early one, is now over; the woods are green, the flowers in full bloom, and already the earth is made ready for the summer harvest.

According to an old Russian tradition, the people decorate their homes as well as their churches with green branches; saplings are cut in the woods for this purpose, and wreathes of flowers woven by the peasant girls. There may be, and surely are, some pagan reminiscences in these "rites of spring"; but they also recall the Bible scene of the offering of the new plants and cereals (Lev. 23:10-17, Num. 28:16).

At the "All-Night Vigil" of Pentecost, the meaning of the coming event is most forcefully projected. As is usual in the Byzantine liturgy, the Vigil or great vespers offers a much fuller illustration of the mystery than the mass itself. This is due to the fact that the celebration actually *begins* at the end of the preceding day. Many Western writers who manifest a great love and understanding of the Byzantine rite often omit or ignore the fact that it is the *Vigil* and not the mass of the Feast which has the greatest number of hymns, prayers, and scriptural readings forming the *proper;* the latter is reduced to essentials in the mass of the day (the troparions and the prokimenons, the Epistle, the Gospel and the concluding prayer of the celebrant). On the Feast of Pentecost the structure of the liturgy is, however, different, as we shall see, the exceptionally solemn character of the feast being marked by a special set of prayers in the Vespers of the day, immediately following the mass.

It would take a long time to present the entire *proper* of the Pentecostal liturgy, for among the major feasts of the Orthodox Church, the *Dukhov Denj* celebration is one of the most complex. We shall content ourselves with giving some of the highlights of this liturgy and pointing out the similarities and the differences which exist between it and the Roman proper of the Feast.

The similarities are obvious, since the event reflected in the readings, hymns and prayers, is the descent of the Holy Spirit as recounted in the New Testament and prefigured or announced in the Old Testament.

However, as we study the texts chosen by the Orthodox Church, we find that they are not all the same as those of the Roman proper, or are arranged in a different sequence. While the Roman liturgy recalls at Whitsuntide the anniversary of the Mosaic law given on Sinai, the Byzantine diurnal office and the mass of Pentecost is filled with the Johannine interpretation of the joyful event, or with the prophecies referring to it.

During the "All-Night Vigil," we have the Gospel of St. John describing events after the Resurrection: Jesus entering the place where the disciples were gathered, when the doors were closed and saying "Peace be to you," then breathing upon them with the words: "Receive the Holy Spirit." The Epistle is taken from Numbers 11:16–17: God taking "some of the spirit" from Moses to give it to the elders. Other passages are from Joel 3:1: "Then afterwards I shall pour out my spirit upon all mankind," and from Ezechiel 36: "I will put my spirit within you. . . ." [20]

At the Mass for the Feast of Pentecost, the Epistle is, as in the Roman Missal, from Acts 2, but with one verse more than in the Western counterpart; this verse 2 refers to the amazement of the people. This additional verse does not alter, of course, the story of Pentecost, but lends it more realism; the people witness the change which has taken place in the disciples and are *astonished*.

The Gospel of the Orthodox mass of Pentecost is from John 7:37–52 and 8:12. This Gospel begins with the words:

> Now on the last, the great day of the feast, Jesus stood and cried out, saying: "If anyone thirst, let him come to me and drink. He who believes in me as the Scripture says, 'From within him there shall flow rivers of living water.'" He said this, however, of the Spirit, whom they who believed in him were to receive; for the Spirit had not yet been given, since Jesus was not yet glorified.

The Roman Mass of the Feast of Pentecost is also taken from St. John, and it also speaks of an event to come (14:23–31), the descent of the Paraclete whom the Father will send in Christ's name. The event is far closer (since Christ is soon to be glorified) than in the text chosen by the Byzantine liturgist. But both texts convey the same feeling of expectation and of certitude, though each is attuned to a peculiar key.

20. Meyendorff, p. 71.

As we go over the Byzantine Pentecostal liturgy, we find, of course, the various hymns, antiphons and prokimenons set in a beautiful and noble pattern. However, this pattern is full of restraint. There is no central prayer to the Paraclete as the *Veni Creator,* Come O Holy Spirit, which marks the climax of the Roman celebration of the Feast. One might say indeed, as we have previously pointed out, that the Orthodox liturgist, just as the Orthodox theologian, is careful not to offer to the faithful a *"special devotion"* to the Third Person of the Holy Trinity.

There *is* a culminating point in the Orthodox Pentecostal liturgy: these are the three prayers read at the Vespers of the Feast, which, as we have said, follow immediately after the Eucharistic sacrifice of that day. These are extremely long prayers (they fill several pages of the Service Book of the Russian Orthodox Church) and are solemnly read by the priest kneeling in front of the altar. They are not, however, addressed to the Holy Spirit only, but to God the Father and Jesus Christ as well, and bear a certain resemblance to the Roman prayers of Rogation. To be sure the priest asks God to grant him and the faithful the gifts of the Paraclete, dispensor of all good things, but he also implores God's protection, help, the remission of sins, and the granting of eternal rest and peace to the deceased. In order to appreciate the wide scope of these three prayers, they should be read *in extenso;* they represent all that our supplications should and can be on the great feast which commemorates the founding of the Church and the birth of the new man called to deification.

Speaking of the major Russian-Orthodox feasts we would, of course, like to know more about the way these important liturgical events are marked in the Soviet Union in the churches placed under the jurisdiction of the Patriarch of Moscow. The latter publishes in its journal a record of the major celebrations; we can, therefore, be convinced that, in spite of the restrictions imposed upon the Church by the Communist government, the liturgy of the major feasts has been carefully observed. No doubt it is precisely in this time, when the magisterium of the Russian-Orthodox Church encounters so many difficulties under Soviet rule, that the liturgy acquires an even greater importance than ever; it is not only the icon depicting the Gospel scenes and the story of salvation; it is also an open book of "everyman's theology" concerning the Mysteries.

The presentation of theological truth through the Liturgy precisely leads to that "very simple and yet very deep piety" of the Orthodox people described by Father Yves Congar. And we find in the publication of the Moscow Patriarchate that this piety is further stimulated by the homily. This form of commentary on the Scriptures (Epistle and Gospel of the day) which has been so strongly recommended and one may say "revived" by the Vatican Council, has always been the most usual form of predication in the Russian-Orthodox Church. It has acquired an even greater importance now, under Soviet rule, since the priest may express in the homily a series of principles based on moral and mystical theology which he cannot teach the laity through catechism or spiritual writings. This author has heard homilies delivered to the faithful in the churches of Moscow and was impressed by the deep emotion and fervor with which the congregation listened to every word of the priest addressing them from the ambo. For this reason, this paper would not be complete without the mention of one of these homilies delivered on *Dukhov Denj*, the Feast of the Spirit, in a church of the Moscow Patriarchate's jurisdiction.

This sermon, reproduced in the Journal of the Moscow Patriarchate, was delivered on Pentecost 1963.[21] The priest who gave it was designated by name as Archpriest A. Vetelov. After having briefly recalled the descent of the Holy Spirit on the Apostles, and St. Peter's discourse which followed this event, the speaker went on to say:

From that day on, all those who believe in Christ receive from Christ's Church the gifts of the Holy Spirit for the struggle against sin and for the growth of spiritual life, of the love of God and of our neighbor. From that day on, the Feast of the Holy Trinity and the Feast of the Holy Spirit have for us, believers, a special significance.

In the days of Holy Easter we are called to arise with Christ, on the day of Holy Ascension—we are called to ascend with Him in spirit to the Heavenly Father, on the day of the Holy Trinity and of the Holy Spirit, we are called more than ever to enter into communion with the gifts of the Holy Spirit.

On all our Feasts, brothers and sisters, we must not merely recall the evangelical events linked with them, we must participate prayerfully and filled with Grace in these events, as having the most direct effect on our own lives, we must reproduce them and live them in our soul as participants. . . .

The Holy Church specially honors today the Holy Spirit—the Third Person of the Trinity. Let us recall that through the Holy Spirit every life is animated upon earth from the beginning of Creation (Genesis 1:2), that in the Old Testament He acted, "spoke" through the Prophets, and that in the Time of the New Testament He grants us His gifts through the Church of Christ: through the hierarchy, through the liturgy, the sacraments and prayers.

Let us then glorify today the Holy Spirit of God for cooperating with us in making us His "temple" (2 Cor.

21. Compare the Prophecies of the Roman vigil of the Feast referring to Sinai.

6:16). "Do you not know," says St. Paul the Apostle, "that your members are the Temple of the Holy Spirit?" (1 Cor. 6:19). . . . And through this cooperation we shall become such a Temple if we are filled with the love of God and man, with patience, peace, mercy, meekness, abstinence, justice, that is the grace-giving gifts of the Holy Ghost. Then, as St. Macarius the Great said, the soul will "cooperate with the Spirit and become the temple of God." [22]

On Trinity Sunday of the following year, 1964, Metropolitan Nicodimus of Leningrad, in charge of the Patriarchal Church's External Affairs, delivered a homily in the Cathedral of the Alexander Nevsky Monastery. This is the heart of Leningrad's religious life and the official seat of the Metropolitan.

The Prelate's discourse, offered on the eve of *Dukhov Denj*, was dedicated to the two parallel themes: the role of the Triune God, honored on that Sunday, and of the Paraclete, whose Feast was soon to begin with the Vigil.

Metropolitan Nicodimus' homily was therefore constructed very much according to the pattern of Archpriest Vetelov's discourse quoted above. More forceful because of the broader theme and because of the speaker's dynamic personality, the Metropolitan's words expressed the courage and the audacity of the Apostles who had received the Holy Spirit. The speaker quoted abundantly from the Old and New Testament, as well as from patristic writings: St. John Chrysostom and St. Gregory. These quotations, given in Church Slavonic, were of an exalted nature, yet simple and clear enough to be understood by the congregation. The speaker recalled among other things the words of St. Sophronius of Jerusalem: "The Apostle received the powers of the episcopate, having been informed by the Holy Spirit who

22. *Zhurnal Moskovskoy Patriarkhiy* No. 6 (1963).

descended upon them and consecrated them as bishops for each of the peoples whose tongue He taught them to speak." [23]

These words, stressing the collegiate nature of the Orthodox Church, also reflect the ecumenic interests of Metropolitan Nicodimus, who is frequently a delegate of the Patriarchal Church abroad and member of the Central Committee of the World Council of Churches.

The study of the homilies delivered in churches open to worship in Soviet Russia and placed under the jurisdiction of the Moscow Patriarchate is extremely revealing. On one hand, they retain an official or semiofficial character; they do not convey the warmth and inspiration of Khomyakov's ecclesiology, nor the theological renewal as it was attempted by Sergius Bulgakov and Vladimir Lossky, living and writing abroad in a free country (France) and still remaining open to free discussion and criticism. However, the homilies, as those from which we have taken our examples, are far from being conventional pieces of so-called pious oratory. They are "audacious" in their way, since they are a direct and unwavering answer to atheism and materialism of official Communist ideology. As Nicodimus recently said about himself and the Church which he represents: "We are not Marxists." But instead of entering into an ideological warfare, the Russian-Orthodox hierarchy strongly and convincingly reaffirms its positions founded on the Scriptures, patristic teaching, solid dogma, and the liturgy whose treasures the Russian Church has scrupulously preserved. Father Congar was right when he brought out the mystical depth of Orthodox liturgical life.

Up to this point, this paper has dealt with the Russian-

23. *Zhurnal Moskovskoy Patriarkhiy* No. 9 (1964).

Orthodox devotion to the Holy Spirit reflected in public worship. Throughout these pages the importance and vitality of the Pentecostal image has been shown as reflected in the icon, the Triptych of the Liturgy, which, in the Eastern-Christian conception is a foretaste of heaven—heaven on earth. Does this mean that all private devotions are excluded from the Economy or play such a minor role that they almost escape attention? To think as much would be, of course, a grave error. For every practicing Russian-Orthodox honors the Paraclete daily in his prayers at home just as he does at Vespers or Matins. As to the religious, whether ordained to the priesthood or wearing a brother's or a postulant's habit, he invokes the Holy Spirit and the Holy Trinity not only throughout the monastic office, in the various prayers, and in the *Trisagion,* but also in his cell.

But as we have seen, there are no so-called "special devotions" to the Holy Spirit. There are no churches or shrines in His name. There are no icons, of course, representing Him, since He is the *Pneuma;* but He may be represented in the form of a dove in icons depicting New Testament scenes: the Baptism of Christ, Transfiguration, Pentecost.

Perhaps, the Holy Spirit's *presence* in Russian-Orthodox private devotions would have remained unnoticed by many, were it not for the extraordinary manifestation of His powers in the teaching of Saint Seraphim of Sarov. This humble monk who lived in the woods far away from the brilliant court of Russia's capital at the height of its cultural development (the early nineteenth century, the age of Pushkin) gave to his people a teaching which he called *the acquisition of the Holy Spirit.* This teaching which, after his death was preserved and perpetuated by a few nuns in a monastery today extinct, has become the mystic way *par excellence* inside Russia and abroad, wherever the Russian-Orthodox in exile have settled or resettled.

Saint Seraphim taught:

> We must begin here by a right faith in Our Lord Jesus Christ, the Son of God, who came into the world to save sinners, and by winning for ourselves the grace of the Holy Spirit, who brings into our hearts the Kingdom of God and lays for us the path to win the blessings of the future life. . . . In acquiring this Spirit of God consists the true aim of Christian life, while prayer, watching, fasting, almsgiving and other good works done for Christ's sake are only the means for acquiring the Holy Spirit.[24]

St. Seraphim's "Conversation with his penitent Nicholas Motovilov, from which the lines above are taken, is a very simple, very "lively" dialogue between a man still attached to material goods and a mystic whose method has often been compared to "the little way of St. Theresa of Lisieux." The surest means to acquire the Holy Spirit according to St. Seraphim is prayer and repentence, which is the prayer and repentence of the Desert Fathers, which lead man to struggle and "empty himself" in order to be transfigured and deified. Actually, this modern saint had a doctrine as ancient as the dawn of Christianity. Already St. Theodore, disciple of St. Pachomius, taught that nothing is greater than "to acquire the Holy Spirit."

Seraphim's discovery, or rediscovery, was that this prodigious task is at the same time a very simple one. He made a point of assuring Motovilov that the way which he would have to follow was a direct one. The

24. This quotation and the following one are from the *Treasury of Russian Spirituality*, translated by A. F. Dobbie Bateman (New York, 1948), p. 275.

climax of the "Conversation" is reached when Motovilov tells his spiritual father:

". . . I do not understand how I can firmly be assured that I am in the Spirit of God. How can I myself recognize His true manifestation?"

Then Seraphim took his penitent firmly by the shoulders and said: "We are both together, son, in the Spirit of God."

And looking up, Motovilov beheld the saint enveloped in a dazzling light "spreading several yards around and throwing a sparkling radiance across the snow."

"How do you feel now?" Father Seraphim asked.

"Unwontedly well!" said Motovilov.

"But well in what way? How in particular?"

And Motovilov answered: "I feel a calmness and peace in my soul that I cannot express in words."

It is not only because of this extraordinary scene described by Motovilov, that St. Seraphim of Sarov has become one of the most popular Russian saints (though canonized only some 65 years ago). It was because of his simple, and one may say *practical* method of prayer, and because of his entire life as a great ascetic, spiritual director and teacher of continuous prayer. His teaching has become an essential part of Russian devotional life because it retells in simple, understandable terms the concept of man's deification through the Holy Spirit.

St. Seraphim's religious experience is typically Eastern. It resembles little the experience of Western mystics, except perhaps that of St. Theresa of Lisieux, who precisely found a new, *direct* way, so different from the complex visions and revelations of the mystics who preceded her. She belongs to the modern age because of her simplicity, and so does Seraphim of Sarov; he not only felt the breath of the Holy Spirit, but also His fire,

His flame, which he knew how to communicate to the men of his time (and of our time) so much in need of warmth, of the Comforter's charisma. He thus completed the cycle of Divine Economy, which the Fathers described and taught in lofty terms and which the Byzantine liturgy glorified in its threefold icon. The hermit of the Russian woods saw it in the simplicity of his heart, filled with the joy of Pentecost, just as did the cloistered nun of Lisieux, dying in her cell.

It seems that both in the East and in the West, the Paraclete is drawing nearer to mankind. For as East and West re-examine their theology and their ecclesiology, the extreme points of opposition gradually fade, while the great Truths of Christian doctrine emerge out of the mist of mutual misunderstanding. This is what Father Yves Congar, the pioneer of ecumenism, meant when he wrote more than a quarter of a century ago:

> All the positive substance of the Orthodox assertions concerning the Church as a communion of love through the Holy Spirit and the mystical body of Christ are also held by us [the Catholics]. For us also, the true definition of the Church is the Mystical Body of Christ. For us also, the Church is a community of mutual love, and it is the Holy Spirit who, inspiring our souls from within is the author of this unanimity in mutual love.[25]

All in all, the idea of *Sobornost* and Congar's concept of "unanimity in love" are nothing else than the *Koinonia* which the Pentecost granted to the Apostles:

> "And all who believed were together and held all things in common" (Acts 2:44).

25. Congar, p. 266.

RENEWAL OF WORSHIP—
A SOURCE OF UNITY?

by David G. Buttrick *

To MANY observers the words "liturgy" and "Protestant" are antithetical, a complete contradiction. And, unfortunately, the image of the rigid Protestant raging against liturgy with words like "arid" and "formal" is not always a caricature. Yet, at the present time, Protestant churches are in the midst of a liturgical renaissance so sweeping that it might better be termed a revolution. In the last ten years some splendid liturgies have been produced by The Church of South India and The Reformed Church of France.[1] And many denominations in America are hard at work: the Episcopalians, Presbyterians, Methodists, the United Church of Christ. Not since the time of the Reformation has such massive liturgical reconsideration taken place.

Candidly, we must admit that the revision of worship

* David G. Buttrick (Presbyterian), Assistant Professor, Church and Ministry Division, Pittsburgh Theological Seminary, published two titles in the Living Age Series (Westminster Press): *Holy Communion* and *Our Worship Action*. He is also the Editor and Writer: *Service for the Lord's Day* (Westminster Press, 1964).

1. See T. S. Garrett, *The Liturgy of the Church of South India* (London: Oxford Press, 1952). For a description of the French productions, see J. D. Benoit, *Liturgical Renewal* (London: SCM Press, 1958).

is long overdue in most Protestant groups. We acknowledge with shame the ungoverned individualism of
American Protestant worship, its inverted "subjective"
mood, its haphazard ordering, its bondage to clerical
whim and clerical voice. The Roman Catholic lifts a
horrified eyebrow at the proliferation and prodigal
wanderings of Protestant worship, and rightly so. But we
must not forget that present day Protestant "free church"
practice would have offended the reformers—Calvin and
Luther—as much as the sensitive Roman Catholic of
today. Though both Calvin and Luther pleaded the unity
of Word and Sacrament, and wished to retain the Sacrament on a weekly—if not daily—basis, the average
Protestant church in America neglects the Lord's Supper.[2] John Calvin went so far as to suggest that those
who opposed frequent (weekly) observance of the
sacrament were of the "devil": and surely the omission
of the sacrament in our churches is "devilish" indeed.

Neither Calvin nor Luther, but Zwingli, must be regarded as the "father" of "free church" worship. For
Zwingli the sermon was the primary means of grace and
the sacrament, though a way of remembrance and an
expression of fellowship, was no more than an occasional
addendum to worship. Adapting a version of the "Prone,"
Zwingli constructed a weekly service which contained
little more than a long sermon surrounded by intercessions, the Commandments, and the reading of Scripture.[3] This custom, exaggerated by the English Puritans
and continental pietists, was the precursor of our American "free church" tradition, a tradition which soon be-

2. See Calvin's *Institutes* IV, xvii, 44, 46.
3. "Prone" developed in Gaul and Germany during the ninth
century as a short vernacular service attached to the sermon in
the Mass and often included "biddings," the Commandments, a
creed and sometimes a general confession.

came predominant. Dr. Howard Hageman describes the result:

> At the beginning of the nineteenth century the situation . . . could be described this way. In some places the historic liturgy had been preserved as a museum piece. In others it had been altered into an expression of something like a least common denominator religion. . . . In Great Britain, the Netherlands, much of Germany, and the United States the liturgy had entirely disappeared. . . . The impartial observer surveying the liturgical life of the Reformed Churches in, let us say, 1820 could have justifiably concluded that it was just about finished.[4]

Though many Protestants tend to regard the Puritans and pietists as liturgical villains, there were other forces which compelled the aberrations of Protestant worship in America. Protestant churches have been impressionable: too easily they have been swayed by cultural moods and by the shifting concerns of theology. So the individualism and improvisational temper of the frontier invaded our worship tradition, as did the "immanentalism" of the Enthusiasts, the didacticism of the Rationalists, Romantic ideas of "inspiration," and the "sawdust" from a thousand revival meetings. Free church worship in this country is in many ways the result of cultural conditioning, is more "American" than Protestant. For this reason it is hotly defended by the "bourgeois" Protestant who guards his ways of worship as zealously as he guards "free enterprise" and "states rights." Nevertheless the excesses of Protestant worship in America are difficult to appreciate and impossible to applaud.

But even before the beginning of the nineteenth cen-

---

4. Howard Hageman, *Pulpit and Table* (Richmond, Va.: John Knox Press, 1962), pp. 58–59.

tury there were stirrings, and since the middle of the nineteenth century there has been a growing impulse within Protestant churches for liturgical reconsideration. Names can be named: Bethune, Irving, Nevin and Schaff, Baird, Muhlenberg.[5] At present there are many responsible liturgists working within the Protestant churches, far too many to be listed. Particularly within our present century have there been major accomplishments. Prayer books have been edited and published, architectural changes inaugurated, liturgical practices reviewed and revised. For example, the Presbyterians who had not had a stated liturgy since the 1600's published prayer books in Scotland, South Africa, and the United States. In this country two such volumes have been issued since the beginning of the century and a third is being prepared. Much of the force of this "liturgical movement" has been encouraged by Biblical scholarship which not only detected liturgical fragments within the Scripture, but provided a clearer picture of the primitive Christian cultus. A renewed interest in Reformation theology has also urged liturgical reform, particularly as it has involved a reconsideration of the nature of the church. But perhaps more than anything else, ecumenical encounter has shaken the infant surety of the American church and has forced it out of its national womb into a wide world where there are many traditions to be reckoned with and many patterns for worship, some richly liturgical. So the American Protestant has begun to re-examine his heritage, and to question his own churchly behavior, and to see himself in

5. See *ibid.*, pp. 60–108; also Massey H. Shepherd, *The Reform of Liturgical Worship* (New York: Oxford Press, 1961); T. Wedel, ed., *The Liturgical Renewal of the Church* (New York: Oxford Press, 1960); J. D. Benoit, *Liturgical Renewal* (London: SCM Press, 1958). These books provide some history of the liturgical movement in the Protestant churches.

terms of an extended historical past. Nowadays liturgical renewal is not a far dream but a present event: it is happening, and happening more rapidly than most Protestants realize.

Now, granted that liturgical renewal is a present fact, and granted that in Protestant churches there is a proliferation of new forms and new orders for worship: what will be the result? Will liturgical revision move the fragmented Protestant Church into fortunate harmony? Or will divergent tendencies within the several traditions become firmly fixed in liturgy and remain to bedevil all plans for reunion? Will our liturgical productions tend to move us toward some eventual rapprochment with Rome? The questions multiply.

To answer the questions, we must consider the real problem. Liturgy is ever an expression of the Church's implicit theology—its recollection of and response to the Christ-event, and its self-understanding as "the Body of Christ." While Protestant churches may well agree on the general shape of the liturgy and may even share some common forms, as long as there is disagreement in theological conceptions inevitably there will be liturgical divergence. The suggestion offered by some Protestants —Dr. Massey Shepherd, for example—that we can unite in a common liturgy long before we resolve our theological difference is, I think, naive.[6] For it is precisely when we come to construct a liturgy that theological judgments must be made. In other words, Protestants must agree on liturgical "norms" before they can hope to worship together in a common way. The most crucial problem to be solved in the Protestant liturgical movement, then, is the problem of liturgical "norms."

Now obviously both Roman Catholics and Protestants reject what might be called "cultural norms." Though

6. Shepherd, pp. 99–114.

there are individual Catholics and individual Protestants who are culturally oriented, the churches must resist the elevation of any current cultural "style" or any current philosophical system to a determinative position in the ordering of worship. The fact that Protestants have allowed cultural factors to dictate the ways of worship has been devastating. For example, I have attended worship in an urban Protestant church where before the offering there was a feature entitled "The Hymn of the Month" followed by something called "The Ritual of Friendship" (members signed attendance cards) which was scarcely an appropriate substitute for the "Pax." Following the offering, the congregation stood to sing (an "offertory chant"?) a single verse of "My Country 'Tis of Thee." This sort of liturgical tinkering is nothing more than a pernicious "faddism." Now we should not say that cultural considerations are irrelevant to the construction of liturgy. Obviously when a Roman Catholic urges the use of the vernacular in portions of the Mass, he is allowing a cultural factor relevance. But, mark this, the norm which motivates the consideration of the vernacular is not cultural but rather theological.[7] The Gospel does have an "incarnational" relationship to culture, but always the Gospel is supreme.

Again, both Roman Catholics and Protestants would reject aesthetic norms in the construction of liturgy, though there are members of both communions who speak from aesthetic concern. On the basis of a rather peculiar theology we might argue that the pursuit of "beauty" in liturgy is an appropriate attempt to "worship the Lord in the beauty of holiness"; but we should be wary. When aesthetic norms are allowed too strong a

7. See *The Constitution on the Sacred Liturgy*, II 14, III 21, 26, 30, 35; also H. A. Reinhold, *The Dynamics of Liturgy* (New York: The Macmillan Co., 1961), pp. 110–120; Charles Cunliffe, ed., *English in the Liturgy* (London: Burns and Oates, 1956).

voice, worship may become excessively dramatic and subjective, a tendency which both the Reformation and the Counter-Reformation opposed. We have only to study the so-called "Gothic revival" in the Protestant Church in America to find a fearful object lesson; or better, we can reread the influential Lowell Institute Lectures of 1927 by Von Ogden Vogt.[8] Von Ogden Vogt enumerates what he calls "aesthetic canons"—unity, movement, rhythm, style, design—and then applies these "canons" to what he describes as "the art of liturgics." So when he must decide between an altar or a table in worship, the decision is made with a cheerful disregard for Biblical precedence or theological understanding and he writes, "Artistically, no other device has been invented, and one might dare to say nor can be, so effective as the altar. . . . The possibilities of helpful worship are much increased by the adoption of the traditional chancel plan of building, where also the choir can be disposed about the altar and share the service as a Greek Chorus shared the movement of the drama." [9] When the aesthetic rules, worship becomes an "art" and a "drama." So the Protestant Church on an aesthetic "kick" shoved tables into altars, crocheted linens, dusted off brass candlestands, and marketed a mess of liturgical trappings. Processionals, recessionals, robed choirs, split chancels all returned in the frenzy of "American Gothic." Now while many of these things may be useful (we shall not comment), seldom were they studied historically or theologically. Ultimately the aesthetic cannot order worship: it may serve but should never govern.[10]

8. Von Ogden Vogt, *Modern Worship* (New Haven: Yale University Press, 1927).

9. *Ibid.*, pp. 115–6.

10. See Reinhold, pp. 79–99; and Cyril C. Richardson, "Some Reflections on Liturgical Art," *Union Seminary Quarterly Review*, Vol. VIII, 3 (March, 1953), pp. 24–28.

Likewise, psychological wisdom cannot be an ultimate norm: both Protestants and Roman Catholics would agree. Yet, Protestants have often confused the word "spiritual" with the word "psychological" as if whatever was inward was automatically devout. Some years ago there was a rash of books which attempted to design orders for worship based on a reading of "basic human needs." In the 'thirties the Boston School of Theology conducted a poll, sampling the so-called "spiritual needs" of Americans and at least one Protestant clergyman argued that worship should be geared to the satisfaction of these "needs": ". . . You have to begin with people where they are and this report of what people feel themselves most concerned about may well give us a clear indication as to the felt needs to which the worship service must minister. . . ." [11] The problem here is that worship is no longer "to glorify God" but to gratify man. Now inevitably worship will have a subjective dimension, a human facet, and may even be analyzed psychologically—why not? But to consider worship simply in terms of human activity or feeling is to miss the point entirely. In both Roman Catholic and Protestant doctrine the initiative in worship is with God, the God revealed in Christ our Lord. Though worship does involve a human response, even this response is quickened by the active power of God through the Spirit. Psychological wisdom is useful, especially in an analysis of the symbols of worship (i.e., words and movements, etc.), but psychological wisdom can never be given precedence as a liturgical "norm."

What then are our liturgical norms? Actually, within the liturgical movement our major concern must be with

11. Albert W. Palmer, *Come, Let Us Worship* (New York: The Macmillan Co., 1941), p. 5.

tradition on the one hand and Biblical theology on the other hand. The Presbyterian *Directory for Worship* states this emphatically:

> Those responsible for the ordering of public worship of God would *maintain fidelity to the aspects of public worship which are seen in Scripture and in the New Testament Church; maintain receptiveness to the historic experience of Christendom,* appropriating for their own such elements from the past as have been found consistent with the right showing forth of the gospel. . . .[12]

Of course, it is God in Christ Jesus who is Lord of the liturgy; and it is He who "calls us to worship" and who, by the mode of the Incarnation, determines our churchly response. But it is within the Scriptures of the Church and within the traditions of the Church, by the working of the Holy Spirit, that we are met by Christ; and it is, therefore, with Scripture and tradition that we must reckon. If there is to be any unanimity within the Protestant communions, or between Protestants and Roman Catholics, it will develop from mutual agreement over the liturgical "norms" in Scripture and tradition.[13]

What of liturgical tradition? Both Roman Catholics and Protestants recognize that, since the time of our Lord, Christians have met to break bread and to take the cup in His Name. Moreover, both Roman Catholics and Protestants recognize that a full "anamnesis" properly involves more than the eucharistic words: it requires a "kerygmatic" proclamation—the preaching of the

12. *Directory for Worship* (1961), Chapter IV, Section 1. (Italics mine.)
13. It may be well to mention that by "tradition" I mean the whole body of churchly event and word from the time of Christ to the present, and not simply the "tradition" of any one Protestant group, or of the Roman Catholic Church.

Word—as a part of the liturgy.[14] Constant in liturgical tradition is a combination of Word and Sacrament. Further we may discern a familiar ordering of Word and Sacrament in liturgical tradition, a sequence that might be called "the classic shape." [15] Students of liturgy can trace this "classic shape" in worship from the third century to the present day in the productions of some Protestant churches, in the Orthodox churches, and in the Roman Catholic Mass. Should Protestant liturgists pre-occupy themselves with the pursuit of this "classic shape" we may suppose that there will be some degree of unanimity in their efforts.

But within liturgical tradition there is not only similarity; there is variety as well, periods of peculiar emphasis, eras when change was great, times of reduction, times of elaboration. In particular, we find differences in eucharistic interpretation not only in the total sweep of tradition, but even within the New Testament (which is, if you will, tradition given priority by right of its immediate relation to the "Christ-event"). So, though liturgical tradition may indicate a general "shape" to the liturgy, it also dazzles us with a wide spectrum of eucharistic interpretation. We must find some means of discrimination. Given tradition, we must have a way of assessing tradition.

Now some liturgists attempt to locate within tradition a basis for adjudging all tradition. Here the trick is to designate a particular era within tradition as sort of a "charisma" and then to weigh all tradition by the chosen

14. See the conclusions formulated by the Third National Congress of the Centre de Pastorale Liturgique, Strasbourg, France, 1958. Published in *The Liturgy and the Word of God* (Collegeville, Minn.: The Liturgical Press, 1959).

15. Here I refer to the famous study by Dom Gregory Dix, *The Shape of the Liturgy* (Westminster: Dacre Press, 1945).

period. Obviously there are Protestants who will locate the normative in tradition within the Reformation period and end by restructuring present liturgy on the patterns of Luther, or Calvin, Zwingli, Bucer, or Knox. Other Protestants may suppose that the English Puritans were the "anointed" and end by embracing an anti-liturgical position. Still other Protestants may seek a liturgical consensus within the whole range of tradition and label this as "ecumenical." Though I cite Protestant examples, I suspect that in the Roman Catholic liturgical movement the same problem may exist, if to a lesser degree. While few Roman Catholic scholars would "anoint" the late medieval developments, some are taken up with Gallican rites, and others hark to the Gregorian reforms, and so forth. There are of course scholars in both the Roman and Protestant groups who seek a "norm" not within a particular phase of tradition, but in a theological understanding of tradition *per se*.

The aspect of the problem which troubles Protestant liturgists is, of course, the dialectic between what we will label "general tradition" and that specific tradition which is contained in canonical Scripture and to which Protestants allow particular authority.[16] Scripture is, for Protestants, a primary tradition by which all subsequent tradition may be assessed. But the problem for the liturgist is that Scripture must be interpreted. A particular, literalistic interpretation of Scripture in the seventeenth century led to the destruction of liturgy. A highly subjective interpretation of Scripture in the nineteenth century urged a sentimental and somewhat humanistic understanding of worship. Now obviously

16. For some Protestant thinking on the problem, see *The Old and the New in the Church* (Minneapolis: Augsburg Publishing House, 1961), pp. 20–51.

liturgical tradition should guard against the capricious or tangential interpretation of Scripture, but for the Protestant it may only guard and not cage the Scriptures. Perhaps the Church must return again and again to the Scriptures, search out the Word of God in the power of the Spirit, stand beneath the judgment and in the light of the Word, revise worship age on age; and perhaps there is no escape from this repeated duty. Liturgy should develop out of a continuing dynamic of tradition and Scripture. While liturgy will conserve tradition of the past, it will always be a "living tradition" expressing the Church's present calling to serve and obey.

Though Protestants do affirm the priority of Scripture in liturgical considerations, they do not suppose that the Bible is a liturgical "guidebook"; it is not. There are no specific rubrics to govern worship provided by Scripture. Nor may we suppose—as did the Separatists—that what is not explicitly provided for in Scripture is forbidden in worship. Such an opinion ends in an absurd reduction of worship or in extravagant exegetical justifications of worship. What the Bible does provide (in addition to insight into the primitive Christian community) is a theology of Church and Sacraments, an understanding of worship, which should be basic to the construction of liturgy. Our task is not so much to shape a common liturgy based on a consensus within ecumenical tradition as it is to frame a Biblical theology of worship which churches may affirm and which may supply "norms" for the production of liturgy. This is precisely why the Presbyterian Church in this country began its liturgical revision with the publication of a rewritten *Directory for Worship*.[17] The *Directory* prints a series of

17. The present *Directory for Worship* produced by the Presbyterian "Joint Committee on Worship" was adopted by the

theological statements derived from Scripture which serve as guide or "norm" for the ordering of worship. Now if there is to be liturgical accord among Protestant groups, it will not come to pass by a proliferation of liturgies which hopefully may move closer and closer to a common order with common forms: this is wishful thinking. The basis of a common liturgy can only be found in common agreement over liturgical "norms." The present task among Protestants, and between Protestants and Roman Catholics, is a discussion and study of liturgical traditions, of Biblical materials relating to the worship of the Church, of the eucharistic "ideas" in the New Testament. Surely the average Protestant needs to be familiar with the great liturgical productions of Eastern and Western Christendom; he should read, attend, and seek to understand the Mass; he should acquaint himself with the liturgical heritage of the Reformation —the revisions of the Mass by Luther, Bucer, Schwartz and Calvin. Moreover, the average Protestant, reacting with ill-considered zeal against what seems to him to be "Romish" interpretations of the eucharist, should re-examine the Biblical materials in which there is such an astonishing range of interpretation. The Protestant may still wish to voice his protest, but let it be a protest from knowledge and not from ignorance.

Likewise, we would urge our Roman Catholic brethren to the same task. It is possible that the Roman Catholic Church is only now recovering from the "rightest" reactions of Trent which tended to restrict and narrow eucharistic interpretation. Might not the Roman Catholic discover within Scripture a broader understand-

United Presbyterian Church in the U. S. A. at the 173rd General Assembly on May 18, 1961. Copies may be secured by writing to the Office of the General Assembly, 510 Witherspoon Building, Philadelphia, Pa. 19107.

ing of the eucharist in spite of the encyclical that
reads ". . . they err more greatly who . . . sophistic-
ally assert that there is a question here not only of a
Sacrifice, but of a Sacrifice and a banquet of brotherly
unity. . . ." [18]
And could not the Roman Catholic consider some of the
recent Protestant formulations regarding the Lord's Supper, weighing them against Scripture and tradition? [19]
Only if the whole Church—Catholic and Protestant—
will come together humbly to restudy tradition and
Scripture can we hope to worship as "one body." I am
trying to say, simply, that patient "conversation" must
precede any attempt to shape common liturgy.

In spite of the fact that we do not at present share
common liturgical "norms," there is an astonishing similarity between the concerns of the Roman Catholic
liturgical movement and those of its Protestant counterpart. Let me suggest some of the major interests of
Protestant liturgists without trying to point out specific
parallels within the Roman Catholic community.

1. *Protestants are concerned that liturgy be an expression of the Church's "corporate ministry."* If, as is
apparently the case, the New Testament words for wor-
ship ($\lambda \alpha \tau \rho \epsilon \iota \alpha$, $\lambda \epsilon \iota \tau o \upsilon \rho \gamma \iota \alpha$ and $\delta \iota \alpha \kappa o \nu \iota \alpha$) are "collective
words," then worship dominated by a single clerical
voice, allowing only passive piety on the part of the congregation, is inappropriate. We remember that the
reformers, intending to offset the individualistic tendencies of late medieval times, urged corporate worship by

18. *Mediator Dei et Hominum,* III, 133. To a Protestant, there
seems to be a more moderate position in the recent *Constitution
on the Sacred Liturgy,* 47, 48.
19. For a recent Protestant reconsideration of Eucharistic
doctrine, see "Report on the Conversation Concerning Holy
Communion in the German Evangelical Church" in *The Ecumenical Review,* Vol. XI, 2 (January, 1959), pp. 188–191.

employing metrical psalms and creeds, and by casting prayers in the plural. So nowadays Protestant liturgists are returning to responsive forms, unison collects, canticles, etc. In the new Presbyterian "Service for the Lord's Day," the oblation in the Eucharistic Prayer is prayed in unison, followed by the "Our Father. . . ." also in unison. After the partaking (of both kinds), a rubric suggests the use of a psalm said or sung, "Bless the Lord, O my soul. . . ." Thus the communion is framed by corporate forms. Of course, there are hymns and sung responses (e.g. the "Sanctus" and the "Benedictus qui venit" in the Eucharistic Prayer) throughout the service. To further express the concept of "common ministry" lay members are encouraged to read the lessons from Scripture, a custom for which there is happy precedent in liturgical tradition.[20]

2. *Protestants are concerned to restore the balance of Word and Sacrament.* Surely one of the reasons for the fragmentation of Protestantism is neglect of the Sacrament, a neglect which may be traced back to Zwingli, to the anxious magistrates of Geneva, to the indifference of the laity so pronounced in the late medieval period, and to the tendency in Protestant theology to interpret the Eucharist as a redundant Word. If, in the past, the Roman Catholic has stressed the Sacrament to the exclusion of a proper declaration of the Word, Protestants have been no less guilty in stressing preaching to the exclusion of the Sacrament. The quarterly communion of the average Protestant church is a grave error indeed. Even as many Roman Catholics are urging a return to Biblical preaching, so Protestant liturgists clamor for a

20. *Service for the Lord's Day* (Philadelphia: Westminster Press, 1964). A revised version of the "Service for the Lord's Day" appears in *The Book of Common Worship—Provisional Services* (Philadelphia: Westminster Press, 1966). A final edition of *The Book of Common Worship* is expected in 1970.

revival of the weekly Eucharist.[21] The Presbyterian *Directory* writes: "It is fitting that the Sacrament be observed as frequently as on each Lord's Day . . . it is seen as a proper part of, and not an addition to, the worship of God by his people." [22] In many of the "free churches" weekly communion will not be adopted without protest, for centuries of defective custom cannot be rectified quickly; but a more regular celebration of the Eucharist is certainly predictable.

3. *Protestants are concerned to restore true Biblical preaching to worship.* This statement may sound peculiar considering Protestant reverence for preaching. But, though the sermon has been a formidable feature of Protestant worship since the time of the Reformation, in recent years it has not always been Biblically grounded. The usual grab bag of topical sermons listed in Saturday newspapers is a symptom of Protestant infidelity to the Reformation principle of *sola Scriptura*.[23]

21. See *The Constitution on the Sacred Liturgy*, 9, 35, 52; also Domenico Grasso, *Proclaiming God's Message* (Notre Dame, Indiana: University of Notre Dame Press, 1965).

22. *Directory for Worship* (1961), Chapter VI, Section 1.

23. A Roman Catholic, Phyllis McGinley, provides the perfect commentary:

Always on Monday, God's in the morning papers,
His Name is a headline, His Works are rumored abroad.
Having been praised by men who are movers and shapers,
From prominent Sunday pulpits, newsworthy is God.
On page 27, just opposite Fashion Trends,
One reads at a glance how He scolded the Baptists a little.
Was firm with the Catholics, practical with the Friends,
To Unitarians pleasantly noncommittal.
In print are His numerous aspects, too: God smiling,
God vexed, God thunderous, God whose mansions are pearl,
Political God, God frugal, God reconciling
Himself with science, God guiding the Camp Fire Girl.
Always on Monday morning the press reports
God as revealed to His vicars in various guises—
Benevolent, stormy, patient, or out of sorts.
God knows which God is the God God recognizes.

"The Day After Sunday" in *The Love Letters of Phyllis McGinley* (New York: The Viking Press, 1954).

Part of the blame must be traced to the liturgical separation of Scripture from sermon in "free-church" orders for worship. In most of the new Protestant liturgies, the sermon is returned to its proper position immediately following the readings from Scripture. Moreover, pericope preaching is encouraged by the production of lectionaries based either on the church year or on some notion of "holy history." While the new Presbyterian service has abandoned the traditional tri-part reading of Scripture (Old Testament, Epistle, Gospel) except as an option, it does provide a comprehensive lectionary on a two-year cycle.[24] And the Presbyterian *Directory* furthers the cause of Biblical preaching by insisting that the sermon "is properly and regularly an exposition of Scripture."[25] The preaching of the Word can never be replaced by mere recitation of Scripture, or by the liturgical use of Scripture, for in the sermon God's Word becomes present address. This was the Reformation position: preaching is more than an interpretation of or a meditation upon Scripture, it is itself true Word of God. Thankfully, the liturgical movement in the Protestant churches is seeking to recover the tradition of Biblical proclamation.

4. *Protestant liturgists are gravely concerned with the Church's calling to intercede for the world.* Intercession is a task in which the whole congregation is involved.[26] Therefore it seems likely that the long "free prayer" offered by many Protestant pastors is not entirely useful. The new French *Liturgique* contains an astonishing

24. The distinction between Epistle and Gospel is largely arbitrary. Not only must we acknowledge the earlier dating of the Epistles, but we must admit that they are as much "Gospel" as the gospels. The Presbyterian liturgy retains an Old Testament and a New Testament lesson each Lord's Day.

25. *Directory for Worship* (1961), Chapter III, Section 3.

26. *The Constitution on the Sacred Liturgy*, 53, which restores the "prayer of the faithful" to the Mass, witnesses to the same concern for corporate intercession.

number of brief intercessions to be used selectively in the Lord's Day worship. And the new Presbyterian liturgy provides a sequence of biddings and brief collects. Instead of the usual salutation prior to the prayers, there is a fine versicle, "The Lord is risen. HE IS RISEN INDEED," to remind worshippers that our intercession is through the intercession of the risen Christ. After each of the "biddings" that follow, rubrics advise periods of silent prayer to be concluded with terse collects. The people respond "AMEN" after each of the collects. In addition to the sequence of intercessions provided in the "Service for the Lord's Day," the completed Presbyterian service book will include a treasury of intercessions for use in public worship.

5. *Protestant liturgists are concerned with the problem of liturgical language.* Presumably the question of language is raised by the fact that the whole Church—the people—is to participate in the public worship of God. And if the people are to participate, must not worship be in a language they use and understand rather than in an archaic "lingo" that has lost meaning? Certainly "vouchsafe" and "beseech" are seldom, if ever, used by the English speaking citizen of the twentieth century. But the problem of language affects not only words we use in petition but also the traditional expressions of Eucharistic theology. For example, the word "memorial" so rich in liturgical meaning no longer communicates what once it did. Today we talk of "Memorial Day" or of "memorial stones" and cannot comprehend the word as it is used in a Eucharistic Prayer. Apparently we must speak our Eucharistic ideas in words that are culturally understood: an awesome task. Language always embodies cultural assumptions, and our language tends to express the rational assumptions of the Enlightenment. Thus, we are expected to phrase liturgical

meaning in a language that is essentially anti-liturgical; to convey faith with secular words. Moreover, the problem is doubly confounded by the fact that our language is presently unstable, reflecting the cultural upheaval in which we live. Since the second edition of *Webster's New International Dictionary* was issued in 1934 more than half of the words then included have dropped from common use, and one hundred thousand new words have appeared.[27] In a time when language is changing and meanings are "slippery," we must employ the simple, basic words of our vocabulary in liturgy, avoiding both the archaic and the transient modern. The French *Liturgique* has managed to accomplish this task brilliantly, and Presbyterians can only hope to have done as well. In any event we must remember that our Lord did not deny human flesh, or refuse the common language of his time and place.

6. *Lastly, Protestant liturgists intend to restore what might be called a proper Eucharistic "mood."* Investigation of the primitive Christian cultus leads us to suppose that the solemn Protestant Lord's Supper with its "heavy" recollection of the passion and death of Christ is scarcely consistent with the Eucharistic joy recorded in the Gospel of Luke (Luke 24:30,36) and in the Acts of the Apostles where it is mentioned that the first Christians broke bread with "extreme joy" ($\varepsilon \quad \alpha\gamma\alpha\lambda\lambda\iota\alpha\delta\varepsilon\iota$).[28] In other words, we find in Scripture, in the *Didache,* and certainly in the worship of the Eastern churches a peculiar festive joy which unhappily has been lost. And

27. See the amazing article by Dwight Macdonald, "The String Untuned," *The New Yorker* Magazine, March 10, 1962.
28. See Oscar Cullman, *Early Christian Worship* (London: SCM Press, 1953); also Oscar Cullman and F. J. Leenhardt, *Essays on the Lord's Supper* (Richmond, Va.: John Knox Press, 1958); and also Cyril C. Richardson, "Toward An Ecumenical Worship," *Christendom,* XII, 4 (Autumn, 1947).

yet, if the Eucharist is, as Scripture indicates, a "Banquet of the New Age" as well as a remembering of Christ's death, we will do well to allow the note of irrepressible gratitude to sound through our liturgical constructions. We do recall the death of Christ in the Eucharist, but never apart from His resurrection triumph, His present Lordship, and the hope of His coming Kingdom. Surely the Eucharist should break into song, should ring with the shout of victory, as a witness to the world of our faith in Jesus Christ who has overcome the world (John 16:33). The new Presbyterian service uses words from the Lukan Emmaus narrative in addition to the traditional "Words of Institution" (I Corinthians 11), to introduce the notion of a resurrection feast. These passages from Scripture are immediately followed by an announcement, "Beloved, this is the joyful feast of the people of God!" [29]

Now obviously many of the concerns of the Protestant liturgical movement are shared by Roman Catholics. Catholics are also distressed by the individualism of popular piety and are eager to encourage full participation in the Mass. Many Roman Catholic scholars have urged the basilican posture for the officiating priest, the use of the vernacular, the offering of the cup to the laity, the renewal of Biblical preaching, and an increase in intercessory concern. That these interests have not gone unheard and unheeded is obvious to anyone who has read the impressive *Constitution on the Sacred Liturgy* of the Second Vatican Council. Surely it is a witness to the work of the Holy Spirit that both Protestants and Roman Catholics should be animated by the same liturgical concerns.

The questions remain: will liturgical renewal in the

29. *The Book of Common Worship, Provisional Services,* pp. 29–30.

Protestant churches urge reunion or act divisively? Will liturgiual renewal in the Protestant churches make possible any future rapproachement with Rome?

There is, I suppose, a move toward "ecumenical" worship in that there is much accord among Protestant liturgists over the general "shape" of liturgy, a "shape" which is to be traced in the elaborations of the present day Mass, and in most of the historic liturgies of Christendom. But while there is surprising similarity in the recent liturgical productions of our churches, there are differences. Some differences are minor—matters of language, of emphasis—but there are other more serious differences; these are doctrinal, having to do primarily with Eucharistic interpretation. The spectrum of Eucharistic interpretation within Protestantism is wide, ranging from those who view the sacrament as no more than a symbol of churchly "togetherness" to those who accept the idea of "real sacrifice." [30] Underlying these differences is, as I have suggested, a difference in the understanding of liturgical "norms"—the weighing of tradition and Scripture. So while Protestant liturgical developments will tend to exhibit a common "shape," beneath surface similarity we may sense sharp distinctions in implicit theology. Should these distinctions force Protestants to deeper ecumenical conversation, we may eventually see solid liturgical agreement.

Of course, liturgical renewal in the Protestant churches of America has encountered opposition (even as have liturgical movements within the Roman Catholic Church). Ignorance and nostalgia are constant enemies. As anti-Protestantism in the Roman Catholic Church has made some liturgical revisions terribly difficult, so anti-Roman Catholicism within the Protestant groups prompts

30. See Pehr Edwall, Eric Hayman and William D. Maxwell, eds., *Ways of Worship* (New York: Harper and Bros., 1951).

stubborn resistance to liturgical change. Within Protestantism we face a massive educational task that members may be acquainted not only with their own Reformation heritage in worship, but with a heritage that pre-dates the Reformation in both East and West. But this educational task may be easier than we suspect. Never before has there been such a stirring of interest among the laity of our churches. It is possible that there will be widespread reception of a liturgy that permits the people to participate not passively, but actively in the dialogue of Christian worship.

The Liturgical Movement in Protestant churches is stronger than it has ever been and may well serve as a useful corrective to worship that has become oddly inverted and impoverished. Liturgical interest may work toward the reunion of the several Protestant "families" and their "offspring," young Protestant groups in Asia, India, and Africa. But whether there can be eventual reconciliation with the Roman Catholic Church is another question. The answer may lie in the success of the Liturgical Movement in the Roman Catholic Church as well as the corresponding movement in Protestantism.

MOTIVATIONS FOR WORSHIP IN PROTESTANTISM

by James F. White *

I AM going to discuss a topic which has not, as far as I know, ever received any treatment. This is the problem of the various motivations for worship, both public and in private, which can be observed in Protestantism. The question I shall treat can be stated simply: "Why worship?" The answer may possibly be so obvious that it can be summed up by Luther's remark: "To have a God is to worship God." Though the reformers wrote numerous treatises on sacramental theology or on correcting abuses in liturgical practice, I know of no important discussion of the reason or reasons for worship itself. Perhaps special discussions were unnecessary. But I think we can learn something about Protestant spirituality by uncovering the motivations for worship as they have emerged or remained as unspoken assumptions over more than four hundred years of Protestant history.

I think we can find some real assistance by borrowing

* James White (Methodist), Assistant Professor of Worship, Southern Methodist University, is a member of the Advisory Board of the World Center of Liturgical Studies. His most recent books include *Protestant Worship and Church Architecture* (Oxford, 1964).

two familiar terms from a discipline which frequently parallels that of Christian worship, the field of Christian ethics. The terms are "deontological" and "teleological." In ethics deontological refers to motivation from a sense of duty or obligation to do what is right, whereas the term teleological denotes a motivation stemming from a desire to accomplish some purpose or end, that is, to do what is good. If the ethicists do not mind, I would like to use these terms in analyzing the motivations behind Protestant worship.

Looking first at the deontological motivation for worship, one notices several different aspects of this approach. In the first place worship may be considered as the inevitable consequence of the recognition of God's love for the individual or his group. It may become an inescapable part of the tribal or community response in which the individual can hardly escape various social or civil pressures to worship if he is to remain a member of the group. The purges of Jehu and other reforming Hebrew monarchs reflect this in the Old Testament. The Test Act of 1673 in England is an example of the same thing in Protestantism whereby participation in holy communion became a legal necessity for holding public office.

But there is a higher ground of obligation when worship is seen as based on divine fiat. Curiously, the Bible seems to spend a great deal more time condemning the worship of the wrong gods than it does in demanding the worship of Yahweh. The forms of worship are detailed in numerous places but I am not aware of actual commandments to worship. There are, however, instructions about offering sacrifice which is seen occasionally as a divine command as in the story of the sacrifice of Isaac. In such cases sacrifice is performed purely out of obedience rather than to accomplish any apparent end.

There are also other rites represented as sanctioned by divine order such as the observance of the Passover, Ex. 12:24. In these cases worship seems to have a deontological character.

Worship with a teleological motivation may have a number of aspects ranging from a desire to glorify God to a man-centered form of therapy. It can be seen as a means of securing God's favor through some form of propitiation as in sacrifice offered to atone for sins. It may become a means of obtaining merit in which the act of worship is regarded as meritorious.

That which is received may become the object of a teleological approach. Worship thus may be looked upon as the opportunity to be assured of God's promises and benefits to the believer. It may become a means of conveying the assurance of salvation or recalling the glory of a past conversion experience. In another context, worship may be performed simply to acquire a sense of security or well-being in order to ease various anxieties. The ends may vary but the motivation in many cases is that of accomplishing some recognized good.

I am quite sure it is impossible to distinguish absolutely between the deontological and the teleological motivations in worship. But they do seem to be poles at times, sometimes more obvious than at others. I should also say that I do not judge one form necessarily any better than the other. Judgments do have to be made but they are usually between a bad teleology and a good one. I think, however, that at different periods in history, one can sort out approximate centers of gravity between deontological and teleological motivations and this I intend to attempt now.

I think one can safely say that both the deontological and the teleological motivations are present in Roman Catholicism though I would in inclined to say that the center of gravity is in the deontological. There has been a strong sense of worship as duty in the Roman Church at least from the third century when Hippolytus prescribed the times at which Christians should say their prayers right up to the *Constitution on the Sacred Liturgy* which speaks of obligation to say the daily office. This sense comes out in the very word office, *officium*, service or duty. It is reflected in the concept of holy days of obligation. I would expect that the average Catholic layman attends mass from a strong sense of obligation.

The teleological is present too, of course. Indeed, this is the area where the reformers so frequently disagreed with other Catholics. Luther uses strong terms in the *Babylonian Captivity* to condemn the ideas about the mass as a sacrifice offered to procure various ends. Neither can he tolerate the mass as a good work used to acquire merit. These, Luther felt, were bad ends but ones which have had extreme historical importance. The good purposes, the giving glory to God, seeking His presence, and acting with the Church did not leave such scars.

I think one can safely say that early Protestantism, like Catholicism, had a very strong deontological orientation though by no means exclusively so. From the sixteenth century through the nineteenth a strong sense of obedience to God's will seems to be a significant motivation for Protestant worship.

It might seem at first glance that Luther, who emphasized so strongly the liberty of the Christian man, would not stress worship as a duty. Indeed, it does often seem to be for Luther a spontaneous matter, a means to express an overflowing of gratitude to God. But Luther is quite clear that the sacraments rest upon divine injunction. In the *Small Catechism* of 1529 Luther speaks of baptism as "the water comprehended in God's command, and connected with God's Word." [1] The command, of course, is given in Matthew 28:19. Likewise the sacrament of the altar is seen as of divine institution in the Synoptics and Paul. In the Lutheran Confessions the note of obligation becomes a bit more pronounced. The *Augsburg Confession* mentions that "this worship [the mass] pleases [*delectat*] God." Luther was quite clear that the forms of worship were not to be imposed "as a law or cause anyone's conscience to be distressed or bound" yet out of love for one's neighbor Christians might "forego our freedom" and abide by set forms "since this external order of service may serve the neighbor." [2] The true Christian, says Luther, has no need of external worship, but does his public worship for the sake of those "who are not yet Christians" and especially for the youth. One is thus free to worship "in the spirit" but nevertheless obligated out of love for the neighbor to use forms in worship. Thus there is a sense of obligation, though in the context of freedom.

The Reformed churches seem to have been somewhat more explicit about the obligation to do worship. Calvin has a particularly striking passage in Book III of the *Institutes* on the divine command to pray:

> And first, indeed, in enjoining us to pray, he by the very injunction convicts us of impious contumacy if we obey not. He could not give a more precise command than that which is contained in the psalm, "Call upon me in the day of trouble" (Ps. 50:15). But as there is no office of piety more frequently enjoined by Scripture, there is no occasion for here dwelling longer upon it. "Ask," says our Divine Master, "and it shall be given you; seek and ye shall find; knock, and it shall be

1. Philip Schaff, *The Creeds of Christendom* (New York: Harper & Brothers, 1919), III, 85.
2. "Deutsche Messe" in Bard Thompson (ed.) *Liturgies of the Western Church* (Cleveland: Meridian Books, 1961), p. 123.

opened unto you" (Matt. 7:17). Here, indeed a promise is added to the precept, and this is necessary. For though all confess that we must obey the precept, yet the greater part would shun the invitation of God, did he not promise that he would listen and be ready to answer. These two positions being laid down, it is certain that all who cavillingly allege that they are not to come to God directly, are not only rebellious and disobedient, but are also convicted of unbelief, inasmuch as they distrust the promises.[3]

Not only is prayer of divine command as Calvin proceeds to show by quoting a number of biblical passages, but failure to pray is a sign of distrust in God's own promises.

The deontological element is present in some of the Reformed confessions. In the *Heidelberg Catechism* of 1563, Question 75 on how the Lord's Supper is "signified and sealed unto thee" is answered: "Thus, that Christ has commanded [*befohlen hat*] me and all believers to eat of this broken bread, and to drink of this cup, and has joined therewith . . . promises." [4] Likewise, the same document describes prayer, as "the chief part of the thankfulness which God requires of us." Christ is regarded as having commanded us to address God as "Our Father."

The *Westminster Confession of Faith*, 1647, contains an interesting statement in Chapter XXI: "The light of nature showeth that there is a God, who hath lordship and sovereignty over all; is good, and doeth good unto all; and is therefore to be feared, loved, praised, called upon, trusted in, and served with all the heart, and with all the soul, and with all the might." [5] As one might

3. Henry Beveridge (trans.), *Institutes of the Christian Religion* (London: James Clarke, 1953), III, xx, 13.
4. Schaff, III, 332.
5. Schaff, III, 646.

expect, this is buttressed with a number of scripture passages. Furthermore, moving away from Luther's attitude, it is also made clear that "the acceptable way of worshiping the true God is instituted by himself, and so limited to his own revealed will, that he may not be worshiped according to . . . any other way not prescribed in the Holy Scripture." The same passage goes on to say that "Prayer with thanksgiving, being one special part of religious worship, is by God required (*iubet*) of all men."

Particularly strong in the Reformed tradition has been a reliance on the fourth commandment: "Remember the sabbath day, to keep it holy." According to the *Heidelberg Catechism*, this means that "I, especially on the day of rest, diligently attend church, to learn the Word of God, to use the holy sacraments, to call publicly upon the Lord, and to give Christian alms." [6] The *Westminster Confession* is of like mind:

> so [God] in his Word, by a positive, moral, and perpetual commandment, binding all men in all ages, he hath particularly appointed one day in seven for a Sabbath, to be kept holy unto him. . . .
>
> This Sabbath is then kept holy unto the Lord [by a holy rest] . . . but also . . . taken up the whole time in the public and private exercises of his worship, and in duties of necessity and mercy. [7]

This rigid observance of the Sabbath became a landmark for much of the Reformed tradition, based upon the interpretation of the fourth commandment as a divine injunction for such practice.

Sometimes one runs into rather far-fetched exegesis. The *Second Helvetic Confession* of 1566 begins Chapter V with the words: "We teach to adore and worship the

6. Schaff, III, 345.
7. Schaff, III, 648–9.

true God alone. This honor we impart to none, according to the commandment of the Lord, 'Thou shalt adore the Lord thy God, and him alone shalt thou worship,' or 'him only shalt thou serve' (Matt. iv. 10.)" [8] The passage in question is the one in which Jesus speaks to Satan after the third temptation. The passage is here directed particularly against prayer to the saints.

The Anglican tradition likewise places considerable significance upon worship as an obligation. There are frequent indications of this in the *Book of Common Prayer* itself. In the Communion Service, the words of the Preface have remained unchanged since 1549: "It is very meet, right, and our bounden duty that we should at all times, and in all places, give thanks to thee, O Lord, holy father, almighty everlasting God." Less well known are the exhortations, one including a passage: "Wherefore our duty is, to come to these holy mysteries, with most hearty thanks to be given to almighty God." [9] The 1552 Prayer Book included an exhortation of similar sentiments which begins: "Dearly beloved, forasmuch as our duty is to render to Almighty God our heavenly father most hearty thanks. . . ." [10] The Catechism in the 1549 Prayer Book, in summarizing the Decalogue, says "My duty towards God is, to believe in him. To fear him. . . . To worship him. To give him thanks. To put my whole trust in him. To call upon him. To honour his holy Name and his Word, and to serve him truly all the days of my life." The 1552 Prayer Book has a rubric binding the clergy "to say daily the Morning and Evening Prayer either privately or openly" just as the daily offices had been required in Catholicism.

The *Book of Homilies* makes it clear that God com-

8. Schaff, III, 838.
9. Thompson, 250.
10. Thompson, p. 275.

mands men to pray to Him both in public and in private. Numerous biblical texts are cited including I Thess. 5:17 which is interpreted to mean: "He willeth us to pray continually without any intermission or ceasing, meaning thereby that we ought never to slack nor faint in prayer, but to continue therein to our lives' end." [11] One finds common prayer sanctioned by the fourth commandment: "God's will and commandment was to have a solemn time and standing day in the week, wherein the people should come together and have in remembrance his wonderful benefits, and to render him thanks for them, as appertaineth to loving, kind, and obedient people." [12]

In the eighteenth century John Wesley could make a vigorous appeal for frequent communion on the basis that constant communion was a duty. In a famous sermon, he argued: "It is the duty of every Christian to receive the Lord's Supper as often as he can. . . . It is a plain command of Christ. That this is his command appears from the words of the text—'Do this in remembrance of me.'" [13] This, of course, is in line with the usual Protestant tendency to base the sacraments on dominical institution but Wesley here extends the text to dictate frequent communion.

In many cases common worship was enjoined by law as a means of preserving national unity. The persecutions, wars, and suffering of the English people in a vain effort to achieve national solidarity through worship were not untypical. Various acts of uniformity, the Test Act, and other vain attempts used national weal as a

11. *Certain Sermons or Homilies Appointed to Be Read in Churches in the Time of Queen Elizabeth of Famous Memory* (London: S.P.C.K., 1938), p. 339.
12. *Ibid.*, p. 361.
13. Albert C. Outler (ed.), *John Wesley* (New York: Oxford University Press, 1964), p. 335.

sanction for compelling all citizens to worship together. Not till 1689 was the unreality of this acknowledged in England.

I believe one can safely say that the deontological factor had a major role in Protestant motivation for worship, at least until the nineteenth century. If the center of gravity did not actually lie here, at least it was somewhere between the deontological and the teleological during the first three centuries of Protestantism.

Turning to teleological motivations, one finds them appearing side by side with the deontological in many cases. But the variety of ends pursued seems to become increasingly complex.

In Luther one finds the benefits of worship most significant. Worship is frequently described as conveying the promises of God. In Luther this seems to come about especially through the preaching of God's Word. In the "Deutsche Messe" he states "the chief and greatest aim of any Service is to preach and teach God's Word." [14] Accordingly, Luther can insist: "The Christian congregation never should assemble unless God's Word is preached and prayer is made, no matter for how brief a time this may be." [15] Worship is a means of hearing the promises of God and for strengthening faith. Though forms are rather indifferent for those who are already Christians, they are necessary to teach the sinner, the simple minded, and the youth to know God's word. Thus worship provides a very important function, for it shows forth God's promises so that all may appropriate them for themselves.

The *Augsburg Confession* speaks of one of the pur-

14. Thompson, p. 129.
15. *Works of Martin Luther* (Philadelphia: Muhlenberg Press, 1932), VI, 60.

poses of the Lord's Supper as bringing comfort to "timid consciences; that they may learn to believe God, and to look for and crave all good things at his hands." [16] It also mentions the effects of nourishing piety towards God. One of the chief criticisms of the Reformation writings on worship is that they tend to make worship so didactic that one almost seems to be using worship as a means of religious education. The charge has a large amount of substance to it but in the case of the Lutheran writers the note of the promises has a strongly existential ring rather than the colder didactic note sounded, for example, in the prayers of John Knox.

Luther, at the same time, rebels very vigorously against what he regards as the dangerous ends in Roman Catholic worship. He is particularly furious at the merchandising of the mass whereby it became, in popular piety at least, a means of acquiring merit. Luther sets out to overcome the "Babylonian captivity" of the mass whereby it has become a good work which man offers to God and to restore to it the sense of a promise given to man by God. He balks at the language of offering sacrifice and says it is God's offering to man instead. Luther insists that this is easier seen when the laity are given the wine as well as the bread. The point here is not so much removing the teleological dimension as in guarding it from ends which Luther considers misdirected.

The Reformed tradition shows many parallels here too. As we have seen already, Calvin places a great emphasis on the promises offered in prayer: "It is strange that these delightful promises affect us coldly, or scarcely at all, so that the generality of men prefer to wander up and down, forsaking the fountain of living waters, and hewing out to themselves broken cisterns,

16. Schaff, III, 35.

rather than embrace the divine liberality voluntarily offered to them." [17] Faith is necessary for prayer, but it rests upon a sure confidence in God's scriptural promises, so copiously documented by the Genevan reformer. Indeed, to fail to seek God in case of necessity is to defraud Him of His due honor and to enter into a form of idolatry, by, in effect, denying that God is the author of all our blessings. A very important end of prayer is to seek relief in our grievous need.

Calvin argues that when one partakes of the Lord's Supper it is to receive Christ as "offered by the promises, not that we may stop short at the sight or mere knowledge of him, but that we may enjoy true communion with him." [18] Calvin them goes on to say that in the Lord's Supper, Christ procured "righteousness for us— first that we might become one body with him; and, secondly, that being made partakers of his substance, we might feel the result of this fact in the participation of all his blessings." Obviously the communicant is aware of the benefits to be procured through rightly receiving the sacrament.

Calvin does make it very clear that the benefits are contingent upon the Word without which there cannot be a "right administration" of the Lord's Supper. "Any utility," he says, "which we derive from the Supper requires the word." [19] Thus the sacrament shows forth the benefits which Christ confers upon us. This is quite in keeping with his general view of the sacraments as means by which God "accommodates himself to our capacity." Baptism too is performed to teach and attest to various things, notably forgiveness of sins, mortification and new life in Christ, and our reception of all Christ's

17. *Institutes,* III, xx, 14.
18. *Institutes,* IV, xvii, 11.
19. *Institutes,* IV, xvii, 39.

benefits. For these reasons the font should be near the pulpit that the benefits may be made clear to all.

The Reformed confessions, like Calvin, also point out various purposes achieved through doing worship. The *Heidelberg Catechism* describes the purpose of the Lord's Supper as "not only to embrace with a believing heart all the sufferings and death of Christ, and thereby to obtain the forgiveness of sins and life eternal, but moreover, also, to be so united more and more to his sacred body by the Holy Ghost." [20] The same document sanctions prayer "because God will give his grace and Holy Spirit only to such as earnestly and without ceasing beg them from him and render thanks unto him for them." [21] These passages parallel the deontological reasons given by the same source.

In a similar fashion, the *Westminster Confession* lists the benefits to "worthy receivers" of the Lord's Supper. They "spiritually, receive and feed upon Christ crucified, and all benefits of his death: the body and blood of Christ being then not corporally or carnally, in, with, or under the bread and wine; yet as really, but spiritually, present to the faith of believers in that ordinance, as the elements themselves are, to their outward senses." [22] The *Westminster Shorter Catechism* of 1647 notes the benefits for worthy receivers as being "made partakers of his body and blood, with all his benefits, to their spiritual nourishment and growth in grace." [23] Prayer is described as "an offering up of our desires unto God, for things agreeable to his will, in the name of Christ, with confession of our sins, and thankful acknowledgment of his mercies." [24] In another document from the same Assem-

20. Schaff, III, 332–3.
21. Schaff, III, 350.
22. Schaff, III, 666.
23. Schaff, III, 697.
24. Schaff, III, 698.

bly, the *Westminster Directory*, preaching receives a magnificent description as "being the power of God unto Salvation" which is performed for "the honour of Christ, the conversion, edification and salvation of the people." [25] Throughout the Reformed documents one senses a balance between the element of command to do worship and the promise of benefits as reasons for doing such worship.

The Anglican tradition can also be said to balance the concept of "bounden duty" with the invitation to "take this holy Sacrament to your comfort." One of the exhortations in the 1552 Prayer Book speaks of the "holy sacrament of his blessed body and blood, the which being so comfortable a thing to them which receive it worthily, and so dangerous to them that will presume to receive it unworthily." [26] In the *Book of Homilies*, a long collection of biblical commandments for prayer appears in the homily on common prayer and sacraments. "To pray commonly," the homily says, "is for a multitude to ask one and the self thing with one voice and one consent of mind." This and the sacraments are vital "to the end that the congregation of Christ might from time to time be put in remembrance of their unity in Christ, and that, as members all of one body, they ought, both in prayers and otherwise, to seek and desire one another's commodity, and not their own without other's." [27] Charity for each other, of course, is only one end of common prayer as well as of private prayer. Similarly, John Wesley finds the holy communion as both "a command of God" and "as a mercy to man." The communion is often, Wesley found, a "converting ordinance" and thus serves

25. Thompson, p. 366.
26. Thompson, p. 275.
27. p. 378.

a most useful purpose for the Church as well as being an act carried out by divine command.

Thus far there seems to be a reasonable balance between the understanding of worship as based upon divine injunction and worship as motivated by the desire to obtain some benefit or promise. Duty and promise seem to be used as joint sanctions in many of the documents of the sixteenth through the eighteenth centuries.

Though there are fewer official documents to go by, the period since the eighteenth century seems to offer a somewhat different picture. The deontological factors retreat and new teleological ones come to the fore. Part of the insignificance of the deontological for this period was, no doubt, due to biblical scholarship which forced a revision of literal interpretations of many texts. The traditional justification for the sacraments as based on divine command (Mt. 28:19 and I Cor. 11:24), for instance, could no longer be held as the actual words of Jesus.

One senses in the nineteenth century a tendency to direct worship toward producing religious feelings in which the end of worship becomes largely giving assurance of a state of salvation. This was perhaps hinted at in Pietism as early as the seventeenth century and is occasionally suggested in eighteenth-century Methodism. But it is not until the nineteenth century that this approach to worship comes to dominate a large sector of Protestantism. A variety of factors combine to introduce new ends for doing worship—conversion, reassurance, and the savoring of a vaguely defined religious atmosphere.

One of the most apparent forces was an American development, the revival system. It must be remembered that contrary to the fond memories of some patriotic societies, the founding fathers of this country were not very godly, not especially righteous, and not particularly sober. One of the most fantastic accomplishments of American Christianity was that of transforming a populace of something like five per cent Christian in 1776 to one where the ratio is now over sixty per cent. Revivalism was one of the most potent forces in accomplishing this extraordinary missionary task.

While giving credit to revivalism for its great accomplishments, it is necessary to look at the effect it had on Protestant worship. It must be remembered that the revival system had its origins on the western frontier. Its most striking feature there, was the camp meeting in which pioneers from miles around gathered for several days of preaching, counseling, and worship. Many of them could not be called Christians by any stretch of the term, but through the camp meeting many were converted. Few of them were tolerant of discipline either civil or religious. We do not have time here to go into details of the effect of the frontier on American religion. But just as the frontier was one force mitigating the stern decrees of Calvinism, so too its force in changing the motivations for worship were and still are felt in American Protestantism.

Many a frontier preacher found that the emotions could be most useful in bringing worshipers to repent of their sin and to be converted. Perhaps some writers have exaggerated the role of the highly dramatic physical manifestations of emotional experience, but the core of the revival system remained the emotional crisis in which one passed from a state of darkness into the glorious and dazzling light of the converted. Much was done to make such an experience possible and one gets the impression that much of American Protestant worship in the nineteenth century was oriented to the end of producing conversions. Here we see a new factor at work. Worship acquired a new purpose, converting those who had not yet had a conversion experience. The same purpose is still noticeable in many Protestant services today which end with a more or less stirring altar call.

I think revivalism has had some profound consequences for the Protestant motivation for worship, particularly as revivalism came to be systematized and introduced into the mainstream of American Protestantism. The man who was responsible for this as much as any was Charles G. Finney, (1792–1875). Finney's "new measures" as described in his *Lectures on Revivals of Religion* were new only in the more conservative East. Finney obviously had no respect for tradition as binding in worship. He was a pragmatist and concerned about means which would work in bringing about conversions. He seemed rather pleased that *"in the present generation,* many things have been introduced which have proved useful, but have been opposed on the ground *that they were innovations."* [28] Finney was confident that if one used the new measures conversions would be produced, a strange contrast to Jonathan Edwards a century earlier who described his revival under the title of a *A Faithful Narrative of the Surprising Work of God.* Finney and others made revivalism into a system and most Protestants in this country are affected by it in every realm of church life.

For the unconverted, worship became a means of "getting religion," of having the essential experience. For those already converted, it became a means of recovering some of the white heat of that moment of conviction. The gospel songs of this period recall the intense sense

28. Charles G. Finney, *Lectures on Revivals of Religion,* ed. William G. McLoughlin (Cambridge: Harvard University Press, 1960) pp. 261–2.

of belonging to those whom God has saved and of reliving the first moments of this new rapture. They often have more to say about what I have felt about God than about what God has done for me.

In such folk religion, often quite happily oblivious of the professional theologian, the chief motivation for worship seems to be the emotional experience it creates. There seems to be little of the sense of worship as an obligation by which one obeys God. Indeed, even the Church seems to be a matter of some indifference, its place easily taken by the immense variety of non-denominational reform movements—W.C.T.U., abolition societies, Bible societies, and countless others. Worship became in practice a rather passive occasion in which one hoped for a conversion experience or recalled his own.

There were, to be sure, vast elements of American Protestantism such as the Episcopalians, a few Reformed groups, and the Lutherans, who escaped the influence of revivalism. These bodies were somewhat aloof from the mainstream of American Protestantism at the time and frequently very critical of it. But strangely enough, they often came to similar results, though for different reasons. Particularly in the Episcopal Church, the 1830s and 1840s saw the beginning of a turning back to the past which revivalism so blithely ignored. The period saw a medieval revival in Anglicanism in some ways analogous to that going on under Guéranger in French Catholicism. One of the keynotes was the revival of medieval Gothic architecture, bits of ceremonial, vestments, altar accouterments, and hymns. To nineteenth-century man it all too often meant a bit of delightful stage setting. Campaigns were waged to achieve "correct" medieval buildings with the congregation kept away from the altar by an intervening choir which performed more and more of the service. The result was that for many Anglicans and Lutherans worship became a kind of pageantry staged in order to produce a worshipful mood for the congregation.

The result, as can easily be seen, is a bit more sophisticated than that resulting from revivalism, but not essentially different. One went to worship to experience a mood of great solemnity and be reassured by the sense of security that was produced.

In either case, one went to worship or worshiped in private in order to get something out of it. Worship was largely dissociated from discipline, which had meanwhile disappeared in many other areas of church life as membership increased so rapidly. It was not always clear what one got out of worship but it seemed to be largely a matter of a rather vaguely defined religious feeling, perhaps an assurance that all really was right with the world.

The same thing happened in personal devotions. Prayer came to be valued for what one got out of it but was ignored as a matter of discipline. As a matter of fact, Protestants increasingly ceased to pray because it was quite often obvious that all too often one did not get much out of it. One serious consequence has been the deterioration of private prayer in Protestantism as it fails to produce the expected short-term investment. For the purpose of getting something out of it, prayer often seems like a poor risk. The concept of an obligation to pray seems almost totally lacking.

In common worship the twentieth century saw much of Protestantism move toward the aesthetic stimulus in worship and away from the less sophisticated reliance on revival methods. Unfortunately the findings of psychological research were sometimes employed to make the experience of worship more meaningful. This was

one contact of religion and science which we might have
done without. For in many cases worship came to be
treated as a means to the end of manipulating the congregation in certain ways. Social crusades, inculcation of
ethical values, personal adjustment, all became ends
which worship was used to promote. Aestheticism became a chief tool in creating the proper atmosphere for
the desired worshipful experience.

The result of a defective teleology and an almost complete eclipse of the deontological factor has been a crisis
in Protestant worship. Right now the biggest problem
in Protestant worship is not the frequency of communion, nor the form of the service, nor even fuller lay
participation, but the problem of motivation: "Why worship?" If worship is done only for the purpose of getting
something out of it and that something is either an
emotional experience or a bit of intellectual guidance,
one cannot help but wonder if tinkering with the form
of the service really matters.

The attendance of Protestants at public worship always distresses us though we sometimes try to justify
this by saying that after all they do not feel compelled.
But I am also concerned about those who do worship
but so often do so only in a passive fashion hoping for
the mood or the idea which will justify the effort of
attending.

The problem of private prayer is perhaps worse though
not so obvious. Bishop Robinson in *Honest to God* describes in frank form the problem of the clergy who find
prayer uncongenial though all the world expects to find
them the experts: "We are evidently not 'the praying
type.' And so we carry on with an unacknowledged sense
of failure and guilt." [29] I do not think any of us would

29. J. A. T. Robinson, *Honest to God* (London: S.C.M. Press,
1963), p. 93.

call what he has to say exceptionable though he is perhaps a bit more vocal in his honesty.

I think, though, that the situation will change and is
already changing in our time. For one thing there is a
much deeper concern in many parts of Protestantism
not only with the forms of worship but a prior concern
with the motivations for worship. The essence of the
liturgical movement of our time is not to make worship
fancier but to make worship a truer reflection of our
understanding of God's dealing with man both in history and in present event.

Much of this will mean a searching criticism of present motivations for worship among Protestants. It is
quite possible that the balance between worship as something commanded and as something promised to man as
it seems to be represented in the historic Protestant
statements will again have appeal. The more I worked
through these documents the more I became impressed
by the degree by which the deontological factors and the
teleological complement each other. It seems that with
the disappearance of the deontological the teleological
factors increasingly degenerate into man-centered concerns which seem a bit trivial compared to the promises
directed to man when the divine imperative to do worship is also kept central. It would seem that a good
teleology in worship may more likely be found in the
company of a strong deontology. At least the lack of a
sense of worship as demanded by one's relationship to
God may be an important factor in the rather unfortunate modern teleology which seems to make worship
little more than a form of therapy.

I would like to suggest that the deontological factor
has seen a rather strong and perhaps unexpected revival in recent Protestantism. This, I believe, can be
seen in numerous parishes concerned with the renewal

of the Church where there seems to be emerging a common practice of considering both public and private worship as part of a covenant obligation which members undertake out of a sense of obedience. We hear of many groups which have recovered a discipline through engaging in covenants to abide by an obligation for prayer and for attending certain services. There is also a rather surprising number of retreats in American Protestantism where worship is treated as a duty.

Such efforts may be of great consequence provided that the obligation does not become a mechanical matter but reflects an understanding of man in God's service. The problem of mechanical meaninglessness is always the peril of the deontological without the teleological. One would also dread seeing a bad teleology coupled with the obligation. After all, the reformers rebelled against that. But perhaps we will see a deeper sense of worship as both something demanded and as a gracious gift given to man. It seems there is good precedent for this in the efforts of the early Protestants.